C-2958   CAREER EXAMINATION SERIES

This is your
PASSBOOK for...

Eligibility Specialist

Test Preparation Study Guide
Questions & Answers

NATIONAL LEARNING CORPORATION®

COPYRIGHT NOTICE

This book is SOLELY intended for, is sold ONLY to, and its use is RESTRICTED to individual, bona fide applicants or candidates who qualify by virtue of having seriously filed applications for appropriate license, certificate, professional and/or promotional advancement, higher school matriculation, scholarship, or other legitimate requirements of education and/or governmental authorities.

This book is NOT intended for use, class instruction, tutoring, training, duplication, copying, reprinting, excerption, or adaptation, etc., by:

1) Other publishers
2) Proprietors and/or Instructors of "Coaching" and/or Preparatory Courses
3) Personnel and/or Training Divisions of commercial, industrial, and governmental organizations
4) Schools, colleges, or universities and/or their departments and staffs, including teachers and other personnel
5) Testing Agencies or Bureaus
6) Study groups which seek by the purchase of a single volume to copy and/or duplicate and/or adapt this material for use by the group as a whole without having purchased individual volumes for each of the members of the group
7) Et al.

Such persons would be in violation of appropriate Federal and State statutes.

PROVISION OF LICENSING AGREEMENTS – Recognized educational, commercial, industrial, and governmental institutions and organizations, and others legitimately engaged in educational pursuits, including training, testing, and measurement activities, may address request for a licensing agreement to the copyright owners, who will determine whether, and under what conditions, including fees and charges, the materials in this book may be used them. In other words, a licensing facility exists for the legitimate use of the material in this book on other than an individual basis. However, it is asseverated and affirmed here that the material in this book CANNOT be used without the receipt of the express permission of such a licensing agreement from the Publishers. Inquiries re licensing should be addressed to the company, attention rights and permissions department.

All rights reserved, including the right of reproduction in whole or in part, in any form or by any means, electronic or mechanical, including photocopying, recording, or by any information storage and retrieval system, without permission in writing from the Publisher.

Copyright © 2024 by
National Learning Corporation

212 Michael Drive, Syosset, NY 11791
(516) 921-8888 • www.passbooks.com
E-mail: info@passbooks.com

PUBLISHED IN THE UNITED STATES OF AMERICA

PASSBOOK® SERIES

THE *PASSBOOK® SERIES* has been created to prepare applicants and candidates for the ultimate academic battlefield – the examination room.

At some time in our lives, each and every one of us may be required to take an examination – for validation, matriculation, admission, qualification, registration, certification, or licensure.

Based on the assumption that every applicant or candidate has met the basic formal educational standards, has taken the required number of courses, and read the necessary texts, the *PASSBOOK® SERIES* furnishes the one special preparation which may assure passing with confidence, instead of failing with insecurity. Examination questions – together with answers – are furnished as the basic vehicle for study so that the mysteries of the examination and its compounding difficulties may be eliminated or diminished by a sure method.

This book is meant to help you pass your examination provided that you qualify and are serious in your objective.

The entire field is reviewed through the huge store of content information which is succinctly presented through a provocative and challenging approach – the question-and-answer method.

A climate of success is established by furnishing the correct answers at the end of each test.

You soon learn to recognize types of questions, forms of questions, and patterns of questioning. You may even begin to anticipate expected outcomes.

You perceive that many questions are repeated or adapted so that you can gain acute insights, which may enable you to score many sure points.

You learn how to confront new questions, or types of questions, and to attack them confidently and work out the correct answers.

You note objectives and emphases, and recognize pitfalls and dangers, so that you may make positive educational adjustments.

Moreover, you are kept fully informed in relation to new concepts, methods, practices, and directions in the field.

You discover that you are actually taking the examination all the time: you are preparing for the examination by "taking" an examination, not by reading extraneous and/or supererogatory textbooks.

In short, this PASSBOOK®, used directedly, should be an important factor in helping you to pass your test.

ELIGIBILITY SPECIALIST

JOB DESCRIPTION/DUTIES AND RESPONSIBILITIES

This position encompasses the performance of tasks under supervision with some latitude for independent action or decision. This work is performed under well-defined procedures of the department of social services in Income Maintenance, Food Stamps, and Medical Assistance; determining and verifying initial and continuing eligibility for Public Assistance, Medicaid, and Food Stamps through the use of agency procedures, automated systems, and/or based on face-to-face client interviews; all personnel perform related work

There are three assignment levels in this class of positions; the following are examples of typical tasks:

Assignment Level I

Determines initial eligibility, or verifies continuing eligibility and reapplications for Medicaid, Food Stamps, and/or Public Assistance via use of agency procedures and automated systems with incidental or no face-to-face client contact.

Receives and reviews all required documents from clients/applicants to determine eligibility for Public Assistance, Medicaid, and/or Food Stamps.

Computes and determines the amount of financial assistance for Public Assistance, Food Stamps, and/or Medicaid for eligible participants.

Forwards case records and other documentation for supervisory review and approval.

Authorizes statistical and financial changes in assistance and/or budgets resulting from information received from active clients and prepares all required forms to effect processing.

Maintains records to provide a continuing history of pertinent action in each case.

Assumes responsibility for substantiating the reason for evaluation in all eligibility decisions.

Prepares reports on activities and makes other reports as required.

Assignment Level II

Performs duties as described in Level I in direct client contact.

Conducts face-to-face interviews with clients/applicants to determine initial eligibility, or to verify continuing eligibility and reapplications for Medicaid, Public Assistance, and/or Food Stamps, Makes referrals during interview for other services; prepares necessary memoranda for referral.

Assignment Level III

Performs duties as descrbied in Levels I and II within a caseload concept Income Maintenance Center.

Maintains a caseload of clients as assigned by the group supervisor. Determines appropriate employability status of members of households of clients/applicants, refers to employment programs, takes required case actions based upon employability coding.

Makes appropriate entries in public assistance case records; provides assistance and instructs applicants; computes budget amounts of public assistance grants; prepares and verifies documentation from clients; takes required actions to provide assistance grants.

Contacts landlords/ agents and/or other agencies/officials to obtain or maintain suitable housing for clients/applicants; processes all housing actions such as rent increases, change of address, rent advances, and relocation.

SCOPE OF THE EXAMINATION
The multiple-choice test may include questions on interpreting and applying rules and regulations to specific problems or cases, and obtaining pertinent data from documents, files and coded information; following instructions and procedures; arranging information in the best or most appropriate order or sequence, including alphabetical and numerical filing; clerical accuracy, including proofreading and matching; ability to perform basic mathematical computations, including addition, subtraction, multiplication, division, and calculating percentages; case load management, including working with others, and face-to-face and telephone interviewing techniques; reading comprehension; written expression; and other related areas.

HOW TO TAKE A TEST

I. YOU MUST PASS AN EXAMINATION

A. *WHAT EVERY CANDIDATE SHOULD KNOW*

Examination applicants often ask us for help in preparing for the written test. What can I study in advance? What kinds of questions will be asked? How will the test be given? How will the papers be graded?

As an applicant for a civil service examination, you may be wondering about some of these things. Our purpose here is to suggest effective methods of advance study and to describe civil service examinations.

Your chances for success on this examination can be increased if you know how to prepare. Those "pre-examination jitters" can be reduced if you know what to expect. You can even experience an adventure in good citizenship if you know why civil service exams are given.

B. *WHY ARE CIVIL SERVICE EXAMINATIONS GIVEN?*

Civil service examinations are important to you in two ways. As a citizen, you want public jobs filled by employees who know how to do their work. As a job seeker, you want a fair chance to compete for that job on an equal footing with other candidates. The best-known means of accomplishing this two-fold goal is the competitive examination.

Exams are widely publicized throughout the nation. They may be administered for jobs in federal, state, city, municipal, town or village governments or agencies.

Any citizen may apply, with some limitations, such as the age or residence of applicants. Your experience and education may be reviewed to see whether you meet the requirements for the particular examination. When these requirements exist, they are reasonable and applied consistently to all applicants. Thus, a competitive examination may cause you some uneasiness now, but it is your privilege and safeguard.

C. *HOW ARE CIVIL SERVICE EXAMS DEVELOPED?*

Examinations are carefully written by trained technicians who are specialists in the field known as "psychological measurement," in consultation with recognized authorities in the field of work that the test will cover. These experts recommend the subject matter areas or skills to be tested; only those knowledges or skills important to your success on the job are included. The most reliable books and source materials available are used as references. Together, the experts and technicians judge the difficulty level of the questions.

Test technicians know how to phrase questions so that the problem is clearly stated. Their ethics do not permit "trick" or "catch" questions. Questions may have been tried out on sample groups, or subjected to statistical analysis, to determine their usefulness.

Written tests are often used in combination with performance tests, ratings of training and experience, and oral interviews. All of these measures combine to form the best-known means of finding the right person for the right job.

II. HOW TO PASS THE WRITTEN TEST

A. NATURE OF THE EXAMINATION

To prepare intelligently for civil service examinations, you should know how they differ from school examinations you have taken. In school you were assigned certain definite pages to read or subjects to cover. The examination questions were quite detailed and usually emphasized memory. Civil service exams, on the other hand, try to discover your present ability to perform the duties of a position, plus your potentiality to learn these duties. In other words, a civil service exam attempts to predict how successful you will be. Questions cover such a broad area that they cannot be as minute and detailed as school exam questions.

In the public service similar kinds of work, or positions, are grouped together in one "class." This process is known as *position-classification*. All the positions in a class are paid according to the salary range for that class. One class title covers all of these positions, and they are all tested by the same examination.

B. FOUR BASIC STEPS

1) Study the announcement

How, then, can you know what subjects to study? Our best answer is: "Learn as much as possible about the class of positions for which you've applied." The exam will test the knowledge, skills and abilities needed to do the work.

Your most valuable source of information about the position you want is the official exam announcement. This announcement lists the training and experience qualifications. Check these standards and apply only if you come reasonably close to meeting them.

The brief description of the position in the examination announcement offers some clues to the subjects which will be tested. Think about the job itself. Review the duties in your mind. Can you perform them, or are there some in which you are rusty? Fill in the blank spots in your preparation.

Many jurisdictions preview the written test in the exam announcement by including a section called "Knowledge and Abilities Required," "Scope of the Examination," or some similar heading. Here you will find out specifically what fields will be tested.

2) Review your own background

Once you learn in general what the position is all about, and what you need to know to do the work, ask yourself which subjects you already know fairly well and which need improvement. You may wonder whether to concentrate on improving your strong areas or on building some background in your fields of weakness. When the announcement has specified "some knowledge" or "considerable knowledge," or has used adjectives like "beginning principles of..." or "advanced ... methods," you can get a clue as to the number and difficulty of questions to be asked in any given field. More questions, and hence broader coverage, would be included for those subjects which are more important in the work. Now weigh your strengths and weaknesses against the job requirements and prepare accordingly.

3) Determine the level of the position

Another way to tell how intensively you should prepare is to understand the level of the job for which you are applying. Is it the entering level? In other words, is this the position in which beginners in a field of work are hired? Or is it an intermediate or advanced level? Sometimes this is indicated by such words as "Junior" or "Senior" in the class title. Other jurisdictions use Roman numerals to designate the level – Clerk I, Clerk II, for example. The word "Supervisor" sometimes appears in the title. If the level is not indicated by the title, check the description of duties. Will you be working under very close supervision, or will you have responsibility for independent decisions in this work?

4) Choose appropriate study materials

Now that you know the subjects to be examined and the relative amount of each subject to be covered, you can choose suitable study materials. For beginning level jobs, or even advanced ones, if you have a pronounced weakness in some aspect of your training, read a modern, standard textbook in that field. Be sure it is up to date and has general coverage. Such books are normally available at your library, and the librarian will be glad to help you locate one. For entry-level positions, questions of appropriate difficulty are chosen – neither highly advanced questions, nor those too simple. Such questions require careful thought but not advanced training.

If the position for which you are applying is technical or advanced, you will read more advanced, specialized material. If you are already familiar with the basic principles of your field, elementary textbooks would waste your time. Concentrate on advanced textbooks and technical periodicals. Think through the concepts and review difficult problems in your field.

These are all general sources. You can get more ideas on your own initiative, following these leads. For example, training manuals and publications of the government agency which employs workers in your field can be useful, particularly for technical and professional positions. A letter or visit to the government department involved may result in more specific study suggestions, and certainly will provide you with a more definite idea of the exact nature of the position you are seeking.

III. KINDS OF TESTS

Tests are used for purposes other than measuring knowledge and ability to perform specified duties. For some positions, it is equally important to test ability to make adjustments to new situations or to profit from training. In others, basic mental abilities not dependent on information are essential. Questions which test these things may not appear as pertinent to the duties of the position as those which test for knowledge and information. Yet they are often highly important parts of a fair examination. For very general questions, it is almost impossible to help you direct your study efforts. What we can do is to point out some of the more common of these general abilities needed in public service positions and describe some typical questions.

1) General information

Broad, general information has been found useful for predicting job success in some kinds of work. This is tested in a variety of ways, from vocabulary lists to questions about current events. Basic background in some field of work, such as sociology or economics, may be sampled in a group of questions. Often these are principles which have become familiar to most persons through exposure rather than through formal training. It is difficult to advise you how to study for these questions; being alert to the world around you is our best suggestion.

2) Verbal ability

An example of an ability needed in many positions is verbal or language ability. Verbal ability is, in brief, the ability to use and understand words. Vocabulary and grammar tests are typical measures of this ability. Reading comprehension or paragraph interpretation questions are common in many kinds of civil service tests. You are given a paragraph of written material and asked to find its central meaning.

3) **Numerical ability**

Number skills can be tested by the familiar arithmetic problem, by checking paired lists of numbers to see which are alike and which are different, or by interpreting charts and graphs. In the latter test, a graph may be printed in the test booklet which you are asked to use as the basis for answering questions.

4) **Observation**

A popular test for law-enforcement positions is the observation test. A picture is shown to you for several minutes, then taken away. Questions about the picture test your ability to observe both details and larger elements.

5) **Following directions**

In many positions in the public service, the employee must be able to carry out written instructions dependably and accurately. You may be given a chart with several columns, each column listing a variety of information. The questions require you to carry out directions involving the information given in the chart.

6) **Skills and aptitudes**

Performance tests effectively measure some manual skills and aptitudes. When the skill is one in which you are trained, such as typing or shorthand, you can practice. These tests are often very much like those given in business school or high school courses. For many of the other skills and aptitudes, however, no short-time preparation can be made. Skills and abilities natural to you or that you have developed throughout your lifetime are being tested.

Many of the general questions just described provide all the data needed to answer the questions and ask you to use your reasoning ability to find the answers. Your best preparation for these tests, as well as for tests of facts and ideas, is to be at your physical and mental best. You, no doubt, have your own methods of getting into an exam-taking mood and keeping "in shape." The next section lists some ideas on this subject.

IV. KINDS OF QUESTIONS

Only rarely is the "essay" question, which you answer in narrative form, used in civil service tests. Civil service tests are usually of the short-answer type. Full instructions for answering these questions will be given to you at the examination. But in case this is your first experience with short-answer questions and separate answer sheets, here is what you need to know:

1) Multiple-choice Questions

Most popular of the short-answer questions is the "multiple choice" or "best answer" question. It can be used, for example, to test for factual knowledge, ability to solve problems or judgment in meeting situations found at work.

A multiple-choice question is normally one of three types—
- It can begin with an incomplete statement followed by several possible endings. You are to find the one ending which *best* completes the statement, although some of the others may not be entirely wrong.
- It can also be a complete statement in the form of a question which is answered by choosing one of the statements listed.

- It can be in the form of a problem – again you select the best answer.

Here is an example of a multiple-choice question with a discussion which should give you some clues as to the method for choosing the right answer:

When an employee has a complaint about his assignment, the action which will *best* help him overcome his difficulty is to
   A. discuss his difficulty with his coworkers
   B. take the problem to the head of the organization
   C. take the problem to the person who gave him the assignment
   D. say nothing to anyone about his complaint

In answering this question, you should study each of the choices to find which is best. Consider choice "A" – Certainly an employee may discuss his complaint with fellow employees, but no change or improvement can result, and the complaint remains unresolved. Choice "B" is a poor choice since the head of the organization probably does not know what assignment you have been given, and taking your problem to him is known as "going over the head" of the supervisor. The supervisor, or person who made the assignment, is the person who can clarify it or correct any injustice. Choice "C" is, therefore, correct. To say nothing, as in choice "D," is unwise. Supervisors have and interest in knowing the problems employees are facing, and the employee is seeking a solution to his problem.

2) True/False Questions

The "true/false" or "right/wrong" form of question is sometimes used. Here a complete statement is given. Your job is to decide whether the statement is right or wrong.

SAMPLE: A roaming cell-phone call to a nearby city costs less than a non-roaming call to a distant city.

This statement is wrong, or false, since roaming calls are more expensive.

This is not a complete list of all possible question forms, although most of the others are variations of these common types. You will always get complete directions for answering questions. Be sure you understand *how* to mark your answers – ask questions until you do.

V. RECORDING YOUR ANSWERS

Computer terminals are used more and more today for many different kinds of exams.

For an examination with very few applicants, you may be told to record your answers in the test booklet itself. Separate answer sheets are much more common. If this separate answer sheet is to be scored by machine – and this is often the case – it is highly important that you mark your answers correctly in order to get credit.

An electronic scoring machine is often used in civil service offices because of the speed with which papers can be scored. Machine-scored answer sheets must be marked with a pencil, which will be given to you. This pencil has a high graphite content which responds to the electronic scoring machine. As a matter of fact, stray dots may register as answers, so do not let your pencil rest on the answer sheet while you are pondering the correct answer. Also, if your pencil lead breaks or is otherwise defective, ask for another.

Since the answer sheet will be dropped in a slot in the scoring machine, be careful not to bend the corners or get the paper crumpled.

The answer sheet normally has five vertical columns of numbers, with 30 numbers to a column. These numbers correspond to the question numbers in your test booklet. After each number, going across the page are four or five pairs of dotted lines. These short dotted lines have small letters or numbers above them. The first two pairs may also have a "T" or "F" above the letters. This indicates that the first two pairs only are to be used if the questions are of the true-false type. If the questions are multiple choice, disregard the "T" and "F" and pay attention only to the small letters or numbers.

Answer your questions in the manner of the sample that follows:

32. The largest city in the United States is
    A. Washington, D.C.
    B. New York City
    C. Chicago
    D. Detroit
    E. San Francisco

1) Choose the answer you think is best. (New York City is the largest, so "B" is correct.)
2) Find the row of dotted lines numbered the same as the question you are answering. (Find row number 32)
3) Find the pair of dotted lines corresponding to the answer. (Find the pair of lines under the mark "B.")
4) Make a solid black mark between the dotted lines.

VI. BEFORE THE TEST

Common sense will help you find procedures to follow to get ready for an examination. Too many of us, however, overlook these sensible measures. Indeed, nervousness and fatigue have been found to be the most serious reasons why applicants fail to do their best on civil service tests. Here is a list of reminders:

- Begin your preparation early – Don't wait until the last minute to go scurrying around for books and materials or to find out what the position is all about.
- Prepare continuously – An hour a night for a week is better than an all-night cram session. This has been definitely established. What is more, a night a week for a month will return better dividends than crowding your study into a shorter period of time.
- Locate the place of the exam – You have been sent a notice telling you when and where to report for the examination. If the location is in a different town or otherwise unfamiliar to you, it would be well to inquire the best route and learn something about the building.
- Relax the night before the test – Allow your mind to rest. Do not study at all that night. Plan some mild recreation or diversion; then go to bed early and get a good night's sleep.
- Get up early enough to make a leisurely trip to the place for the test – This way unforeseen events, traffic snarls, unfamiliar buildings, etc. will not upset you.
- Dress comfortably – A written test is not a fashion show. You will be known by number and not by name, so wear something comfortable.

- Leave excess paraphernalia at home – Shopping bags and odd bundles will get in your way. You need bring only the items mentioned in the official notice you received; usually everything you need is provided. Do not bring reference books to the exam. They will only confuse those last minutes and be taken away from you when in the test room.
- Arrive somewhat ahead of time – If because of transportation schedules you must get there very early, bring a newspaper or magazine to take your mind off yourself while waiting.
- Locate the examination room – When you have found the proper room, you will be directed to the seat or part of the room where you will sit. Sometimes you are given a sheet of instructions to read while you are waiting. Do not fill out any forms until you are told to do so; just read them and be prepared.
- Relax and prepare to listen to the instructions
- If you have any physical problem that may keep you from doing your best, be sure to tell the test administrator. If you are sick or in poor health, you really cannot do your best on the exam. You can come back and take the test some other time.

VII. AT THE TEST

The day of the test is here and you have the test booklet in your hand. The temptation to get going is very strong. Caution! There is more to success than knowing the right answers. You must know how to identify your papers and understand variations in the type of short-answer question used in this particular examination. Follow these suggestions for maximum results from your efforts:

1) Cooperate with the monitor
The test administrator has a duty to create a situation in which you can be as much at ease as possible. He will give instructions, tell you when to begin, check to see that you are marking your answer sheet correctly, and so on. He is not there to guard you, although he will see that your competitors do not take unfair advantage. He wants to help you do your best.

2) Listen to all instructions
Don't jump the gun! Wait until you understand all directions. In most civil service tests you get more time than you need to answer the questions. So don't be in a hurry. Read each word of instructions until you clearly understand the meaning. Study the examples, listen to all announcements and follow directions. Ask questions if you do not understand what to do.

3) Identify your papers
Civil service exams are usually identified by number only. You will be assigned a number; you must not put your name on your test papers. Be sure to copy your number correctly. Since more than one exam may be given, copy your exact examination title.

4) Plan your time
Unless you are told that a test is a "speed" or "rate of work" test, speed itself is usually not important. Time enough to answer all the questions will be provided, but this does not mean that you have all day. An overall time limit has been set. Divide the total time (in minutes) by the number of questions to determine the approximate time you have for each question.

5) Do not linger over difficult questions

If you come across a difficult question, mark it with a paper clip (useful to have along) and come back to it when you have been through the booklet. One caution if you do this – be sure to skip a number on your answer sheet as well. Check often to be sure that you have not lost your place and that you are marking in the row numbered the same as the question you are answering.

6) Read the questions

Be sure you know what the question asks! Many capable people are unsuccessful because they failed to *read* the questions correctly.

7) Answer all questions

Unless you have been instructed that a penalty will be deducted for incorrect answers, it is better to guess than to omit a question.

8) Speed tests

It is often better NOT to guess on speed tests. It has been found that on timed tests people are tempted to spend the last few seconds before time is called in marking answers at random – without even reading them – in the hope of picking up a few extra points. To discourage this practice, the instructions may warn you that your score will be "corrected" for guessing. That is, a penalty will be applied. The incorrect answers will be deducted from the correct ones, or some other penalty formula will be used.

9) Review your answers

If you finish before time is called, go back to the questions you guessed or omitted to give them further thought. Review other answers if you have time.

10) Return your test materials

If you are ready to leave before others have finished or time is called, take ALL your materials to the monitor and leave quietly. Never take any test material with you. The monitor can discover whose papers are not complete, and taking a test booklet may be grounds for disqualification.

VIII. EXAMINATION TECHNIQUES

1) Read the general instructions carefully. These are usually printed on the first page of the exam booklet. As a rule, these instructions refer to the timing of the examination; the fact that you should not start work until the signal and must stop work at a signal, etc. If there are any *special* instructions, such as a choice of questions to be answered, make sure that you note this instruction carefully.

2) When you are ready to start work on the examination, that is as soon as the signal has been given, read the instructions to each question booklet, underline any key words or phrases, such as *least, best, outline, describe* and the like. In this way you will tend to answer as requested rather than discover on reviewing your paper that you *listed without describing*, that you selected the *worst* choice rather than the *best* choice, etc.

3) If the examination is of the objective or multiple-choice type – that is, each question will also give a series of possible answers: A, B, C or D, and you are called upon to select the best answer and write the letter next to that answer on your answer paper – it is advisable to start answering each question in turn. There may be anywhere from 50 to 100 such questions in the three or four hours allotted and you can see how much time would be taken if you read through all the questions before beginning to answer any. Furthermore, if you come across a question or group of questions which you know would be difficult to answer, it would undoubtedly affect your handling of all the other questions.

4) If the examination is of the essay type and contains but a few questions, it is a moot point as to whether you should read all the questions before starting to answer any one. Of course, if you are given a choice – say five out of seven and the like – then it is essential to read all the questions so you can eliminate the two that are most difficult. If, however, you are asked to answer all the questions, there may be danger in trying to answer the easiest one first because you may find that you will spend too much time on it. The best technique is to answer the first question, then proceed to the second, etc.

5) Time your answers. Before the exam begins, write down the time it started, then add the time allowed for the examination and write down the time it must be completed, then divide the time available somewhat as follows:
   - If 3-1/2 hours are allowed, that would be 210 minutes. If you have 80 objective-type questions, that would be an average of 2-1/2 minutes per question. Allow yourself no more than 2 minutes per question, or a total of 160 minutes, which will permit about 50 minutes to review.
   - If for the time allotment of 210 minutes there are 7 essay questions to answer, that would average about 30 minutes a question. Give yourself only 25 minutes per question so that you have about 35 minutes to review.

6) The most important instruction is to *read each question* and make sure you know what is wanted. The second most important instruction is to *time yourself properly* so that you answer every question. The third most important instruction is to *answer every question*. Guess if you have to but include something for each question. Remember that you will receive no credit for a blank and will probably receive some credit if you write something in answer to an essay question. If you guess a letter – say "B" for a multiple-choice question – you may have guessed right. If you leave a blank as an answer to a multiple-choice question, the examiners may respect your feelings but it will not add a point to your score. Some exams may penalize you for wrong answers, so in such cases *only*, you may not want to guess unless you have some basis for your answer.

7) Suggestions
   a. Objective-type questions
      1. Examine the question booklet for proper sequence of pages and questions
      2. Read all instructions carefully
      3. Skip any question which seems too difficult; return to it after all other questions have been answered
      4. Apportion your time properly; do not spend too much time on any single question or group of questions

5. Note and underline key words – *all, most, fewest, least, best, worst, same, opposite,* etc.
6. Pay particular attention to negatives
7. Note unusual option, e.g., unduly long, short, complex, different or similar in content to the body of the question
8. Observe the use of "hedging" words – *probably, may, most likely,* etc.
9. Make sure that your answer is put next to the same number as the question
10. Do not second-guess unless you have good reason to believe the second answer is definitely more correct
11. Cross out original answer if you decide another answer is more accurate; do not erase until you are ready to hand your paper in
12. Answer all questions; guess unless instructed otherwise
13. Leave time for review

b. Essay questions
1. Read each question carefully
2. Determine exactly what is wanted. Underline key words or phrases.
3. Decide on outline or paragraph answer
4. Include many different points and elements unless asked to develop any one or two points or elements
5. Show impartiality by giving pros and cons unless directed to select one side only
6. Make and write down any assumptions you find necessary to answer the questions
7. Watch your English, grammar, punctuation and choice of words
8. Time your answers; don't crowd material

8) Answering the essay question

Most essay questions can be answered by framing the specific response around several key words or ideas. Here are a few such key words or ideas:

M's: manpower, materials, methods, money, management
P's: purpose, program, policy, plan, procedure, practice, problems, pitfalls, personnel, public relations

a. Six basic steps in handling problems:
1. Preliminary plan and background development
2. Collect information, data and facts
3. Analyze and interpret information, data and facts
4. Analyze and develop solutions as well as make recommendations
5. Prepare report and sell recommendations
6. Install recommendations and follow up effectiveness

b. Pitfalls to avoid
1. *Taking things for granted* – A statement of the situation does not necessarily imply that each of the elements is necessarily true; for example, a complaint may be invalid and biased so that all that can be taken for granted is that a complaint has been registered

2. *Considering only one side of a situation* – Wherever possible, indicate several alternatives and then point out the reasons you selected the best one
3. *Failing to indicate follow up* – Whenever your answer indicates action on your part, make certain that you will take proper follow-up action to see how successful your recommendations, procedures or actions turn out to be
4. *Taking too long in answering any single question* – Remember to time your answers properly

IX. AFTER THE TEST

Scoring procedures differ in detail among civil service jurisdictions although the general principles are the same. Whether the papers are hand-scored or graded by machine we have described, they are nearly always graded by number. That is, the person who marks the paper knows only the number – never the name – of the applicant. Not until all the papers have been graded will they be matched with names. If other tests, such as training and experience or oral interview ratings have been given, scores will be combined. Different parts of the examination usually have different weights. For example, the written test might count 60 percent of the final grade, and a rating of training and experience 40 percent. In many jurisdictions, veterans will have a certain number of points added to their grades.

After the final grade has been determined, the names are placed in grade order and an eligible list is established. There are various methods for resolving ties between those who get the same final grade – probably the most common is to place first the name of the person whose application was received first. Job offers are made from the eligible list in the order the names appear on it. You will be notified of your grade and your rank as soon as all these computations have been made. This will be done as rapidly as possible.

People who are found to meet the requirements in the announcement are called "eligibles." Their names are put on a list of eligible candidates. An eligible's chances of getting a job depend on how high he stands on this list and how fast agencies are filling jobs from the list.

When a job is to be filled from a list of eligibles, the agency asks for the names of people on the list of eligibles for that job. When the civil service commission receives this request, it sends to the agency the names of the three people highest on this list. Or, if the job to be filled has specialized requirements, the office sends the agency the names of the top three persons who meet these requirements from the general list.

The appointing officer makes a choice from among the three people whose names were sent to him. If the selected person accepts the appointment, the names of the others are put back on the list to be considered for future openings.

That is the rule in hiring from all kinds of eligible lists, whether they are for typist, carpenter, chemist, or something else. For every vacancy, the appointing officer has his choice of any one of the top three eligibles on the list. This explains why the person whose name is on top of the list sometimes does not get an appointment when some of the persons lower on the list do. If the appointing officer chooses the second or third eligible, the No. 1 eligible does not get a job at once, but stays on the list until he is appointed or the list is terminated.

X. HOW TO PASS THE INTERVIEW TEST

The examination for which you applied requires an oral interview test. You have already taken the written test and you are now being called for the interview test – the final part of the formal examination.

You may think that it is not possible to prepare for an interview test and that there are no procedures to follow during an interview. Our purpose is to point out some things you can do in advance that will help you and some good rules to follow and pitfalls to avoid while you are being interviewed.

What is an interview supposed to test?

The written examination is designed to test the technical knowledge and competence of the candidate; the oral is designed to evaluate intangible qualities, not readily measured otherwise, and to establish a list showing the relative fitness of each candidate – as measured against his competitors – for the position sought. Scoring is not on the basis of "right" and "wrong," but on a sliding scale of values ranging from "not passable" to "outstanding." As a matter of fact, it is possible to achieve a relatively low score without a single "incorrect" answer because of evident weakness in the qualities being measured.

Occasionally, an examination may consist entirely of an oral test – either an individual or a group oral. In such cases, information is sought concerning the technical knowledges and abilities of the candidate, since there has been no written examination for this purpose. More commonly, however, an oral test is used to supplement a written examination.

Who conducts interviews?

The composition of oral boards varies among different jurisdictions. In nearly all, a representative of the personnel department serves as chairman. One of the members of the board may be a representative of the department in which the candidate would work. In some cases, "outside experts" are used, and, frequently, a businessman or some other representative of the general public is asked to serve. Labor and management or other special groups may be represented. The aim is to secure the services of experts in the appropriate field.

However the board is composed, it is a good idea (and not at all improper or unethical) to ascertain in advance of the interview who the members are and what groups they represent. When you are introduced to them, you will have some idea of their backgrounds and interests, and at least you will not stutter and stammer over their names.

What should be done before the interview?

While knowledge about the board members is useful and takes some of the surprise element out of the interview, there is other preparation which is more substantive. It *is* possible to prepare for an oral interview – in several ways:

1) Keep a copy of your application and review it carefully before the interview

This may be the only document before the oral board, and the starting point of the interview. Know what education and experience you have listed there, and the sequence and dates of all of it. Sometimes the board will ask you to review the highlights of your experience for them; you should not have to hem and haw doing it.

2) Study the class specification and the examination announcement

Usually, the oral board has one or both of these to guide them. The qualities, characteristics or knowledges required by the position sought are stated in these documents. They offer valuable clues as to the nature of the oral interview. For example, if the job involves supervisory responsibilities, the announcement will usually indicate that knowledge of modern supervisory methods and the qualifications of the candidate as a supervisor will be tested. If so, you can expect such questions, frequently in the form of a hypothetical situation which you are expected to solve. NEVER go into an oral without knowledge of the duties and responsibilities of the job you seek.

3) Think through each qualification required

Try to visualize the kind of questions you would ask if you were a board member. How well could you answer them? Try especially to appraise your own knowledge and background in each area, *measured against the job sought*, and identify any areas in which you are weak. Be critical and realistic – do not flatter yourself.

4) Do some general reading in areas in which you feel you may be weak

For example, if the job involves supervision and your past experience has NOT, some general reading in supervisory methods and practices, particularly in the field of human relations, might be useful. Do NOT study agency procedures or detailed manuals. The oral board will be testing your understanding and capacity, not your memory.

5) Get a good night's sleep and watch your general health and mental attitude

You will want a clear head at the interview. Take care of a cold or any other minor ailment, and of course, no hangovers.

What should be done on the day of the interview?

Now comes the day of the interview itself. Give yourself plenty of time to get there. Plan to arrive somewhat ahead of the scheduled time, particularly if your appointment is in the fore part of the day. If a previous candidate fails to appear, the board might be ready for you a bit early. By early afternoon an oral board is almost invariably behind schedule if there are many candidates, and you may have to wait. Take along a book or magazine to read, or your application to review, but leave any extraneous material in the waiting room when you go in for your interview. In any event, relax and compose yourself.

The matter of dress is important. The board is forming impressions about you – from your experience, your manners, your attitude, and your appearance. Give your personal appearance careful attention. Dress your best, but not your flashiest. Choose conservative, appropriate clothing, and be sure it is immaculate. This is a business interview, and your appearance should indicate that you regard it as such. Besides, being well groomed and properly dressed will help boost your confidence.

Sooner or later, someone will call your name and escort you into the interview room. *This is it.* From here on you are on your own. It is too late for any more preparation. But remember, you asked for this opportunity to prove your fitness, and you are here because your request was granted.

What happens when you go in?

The usual sequence of events will be as follows: The clerk (who is often the board stenographer) will introduce you to the chairman of the oral board, who will introduce you to the other members of the board. Acknowledge the introductions before you sit down. Do not be surprised if you find a microphone facing you or a stenotypist sitting by. Oral interviews are usually recorded in the event of an appeal or other review.

Usually the chairman of the board will open the interview by reviewing the highlights of your education and work experience from your application – primarily for the benefit of the other members of the board, as well as to get the material into the record. Do not interrupt or comment unless there is an error or significant misinterpretation; if that is the case, do not hesitate. But do not quibble about insignificant matters. Also, he will usually ask you some question about your education, experience or your present job – partly to get you to start talking and to establish the interviewing "rapport." He may start the actual questioning, or turn it over to one of the other members. Frequently, each member undertakes the questioning on a particular area, one in which he is perhaps most competent, so you can expect each member to participate in the examination. Because time is limited, you may also expect some rather abrupt switches in the direction the questioning takes, so do not be upset by it. Normally, a board member will not pursue a single line of questioning unless he discovers a particular strength or weakness.

After each member has participated, the chairman will usually ask whether any member has any further questions, then will ask you if you have anything you wish to add. Unless you are expecting this question, it may floor you. Worse, it may start you off on an extended, extemporaneous speech. The board is not usually seeking more information. The question is principally to offer you a last opportunity to present further qualifications or to indicate that you have nothing to add. So, if you feel that a significant qualification or characteristic has been overlooked, it is proper to point it out in a sentence or so. Do not compliment the board on the thoroughness of their examination – they have been sketchy, and you know it. If you wish, merely say, "No thank you, I have nothing further to add." This is a point where you can "talk yourself out" of a good impression or fail to present an important bit of information. Remember, *you close the interview yourself*.

The chairman will then say, "That is all, Mr. _____, thank you." Do not be startled; the interview is over, and quicker than you think. Thank him, gather your belongings and take your leave. Save your sigh of relief for the other side of the door.

How to put your best foot forward

Throughout this entire process, you may feel that the board individually and collectively is trying to pierce your defenses, seek out your hidden weaknesses and embarrass and confuse you. Actually, this is not true. They are obliged to make an appraisal of your qualifications for the job you are seeking, and they want to see you in your best light. Remember, they must interview all candidates and a non-cooperative candidate may become a failure in spite of their best efforts to bring out his qualifications. Here are 15 suggestions that will help you:

1) Be natural – Keep your attitude confident, not cocky

If you are not confident that you can do the job, do not expect the board to be. Do not apologize for your weaknesses, try to bring out your strong points. The board is interested in a positive, not negative, presentation. Cockiness will antagonize any board member and make him wonder if you are covering up a weakness by a false show of strength.

2) Get comfortable, but don't lounge or sprawl

Sit erectly but not stiffly. A careless posture may lead the board to conclude that you are careless in other things, or at least that you are not impressed by the importance of the occasion. Either conclusion is natural, even if incorrect. Do not fuss with your clothing, a pencil or an ashtray. Your hands may occasionally be useful to emphasize a point; do not let them become a point of distraction.

3) Do not wisecrack or make small talk

This is a serious situation, and your attitude should show that you consider it as such. Further, the time of the board is limited – they do not want to waste it, and neither should you.

4) Do not exaggerate your experience or abilities

In the first place, from information in the application or other interviews and sources, the board may know more about you than you think. Secondly, you probably will not get away with it. An experienced board is rather adept at spotting such a situation, so do not take the chance.

5) If you know a board member, do not make a point of it, yet do not hide it

Certainly you are not fooling him, and probably not the other members of the board. Do not try to take advantage of your acquaintanceship – it will probably do you little good.

6) Do not dominate the interview

Let the board do that. They will give you the clues – do not assume that you have to do all the talking. Realize that the board has a number of questions to ask you, and do not try to take up all the interview time by showing off your extensive knowledge of the answer to the first one.

7) Be attentive

You only have 20 minutes or so, and you should keep your attention at its sharpest throughout. When a member is addressing a problem or question to you, give him your undivided attention. Address your reply principally to him, but do not exclude the other board members.

8) Do not interrupt

A board member may be stating a problem for you to analyze. He will ask you a question when the time comes. Let him state the problem, and wait for the question.

9) Make sure you understand the question

Do not try to answer until you are sure what the question is. If it is not clear, restate it in your own words or ask the board member to clarify it for you. However, do not haggle about minor elements.

10) Reply promptly but not hastily

A common entry on oral board rating sheets is "candidate responded readily," or "candidate hesitated in replies." Respond as promptly and quickly as you can, but do not jump to a hasty, ill-considered answer.

11) Do not be peremptory in your answers

A brief answer is proper – but do not fire your answer back. That is a losing game from your point of view. The board member can probably ask questions much faster than you can answer them.

12) Do not try to create the answer you think the board member wants

He is interested in what kind of mind you have and how it works – not in playing games. Furthermore, he can usually spot this practice and will actually grade you down on it.

13) Do not switch sides in your reply merely to agree with a board member

Frequently, a member will take a contrary position merely to draw you out and to see if you are willing and able to defend your point of view. Do not start a debate, yet do not surrender a good position. If a position is worth taking, it is worth defending.

14) Do not be afraid to admit an error in judgment if you are shown to be wrong

The board knows that you are forced to reply without any opportunity for careful consideration. Your answer may be demonstrably wrong. If so, admit it and get on with the interview.

15) Do not dwell at length on your present job

The opening question may relate to your present assignment. Answer the question but do not go into an extended discussion. You are being examined for a *new* job, not your present one. As a matter of fact, try to phrase ALL your answers in terms of the job for which you are being examined.

Basis of Rating

Probably you will forget most of these "do's" and "don'ts" when you walk into the oral interview room. Even remembering them all will not ensure you a passing grade. Perhaps you did not have the qualifications in the first place. But remembering them will help you to put your best foot forward, without treading on the toes of the board members.

Rumor and popular opinion to the contrary notwithstanding, an oral board wants you to make the best appearance possible. They know you are under pressure – but they also want to see how you respond to it as a guide to what your reaction would be under the pressures of the job you seek. They will be influenced by the degree of poise you display, the personal traits you show and the manner in which you respond.

ABOUT THIS BOOK

This book contains tests divided into Examination Sections. Go through each test, answering every question in the margin. We have also attached a sample answer sheet at the back of the book that can be removed and used. At the end of each test look at the answer key and check your answers. On the ones you got wrong, look at the right answer choice and learn. Do not fill in the answers first. Do not memorize the questions and answers, but understand the answer and principles involved. On your test, the questions will likely be different from the samples. Questions are changed and new ones added. If you understand these past questions you should have success with any changes that arise. Tests may consist of several types of questions. We have additional books on each subject should more study be advisable or necessary for you. Finally, the more you study, the better prepared you will be. This book is intended to be the last thing you study before you walk into the examination room. Prior study of relevant texts is also recommended. NLC publishes some of these in our Fundamental Series. Knowledge and good sense are important factors in passing your exam. Good luck also helps. So now study this Passbook, absorb the material contained within and take that knowledge into the examination. Then do your best to pass that exam.

EXAMINATION SECTION

EXAMINATION SECTION
TEST 1

DIRECTIONS: Each question or incomplete statement is followed by several suggested answers or completions. Select the one that BEST answers the question or completes the statement. *PRINT THE LETTER OF THE CORRECT ANSWER IN THE SPACE AT THE RIGHT.*

1. The purpose of an ethnic survey of city employees is to determine 1._____

    A. the degree of *ethnic group identity* among city employees belonging to various minority groups
    B. whether there has been job discrimination by city agencies against minority groups
    C. the basis for the establishment of quotas which would guarantee jobs to a certain number of minority group members
    D. a method of strengthening the merit system through establishment of discretionary hiring practices for minority group members

2. Of the following, an important purpose of the separation of the functions of income maintenance and social services in the Department of Social Services is to 2._____

    A. give caseworkers more time to provide services and counseling to welfare families and individuals
    B. eliminate investigation of all families and individuals applying for public assistance
    C. enable the Department of Social Services to implement the state-mandated program of check pickup at the State Employment Service
    D. facilitate decentralization of the allocation of funds for services

3. Changes in the Food Stamp Program resulted in 3._____

    A. *raising* both the maximum income for non-public assistance families who would be eligible to purchase stamps and the bonus for families already participating, but also raising the cost of the stamps
    B. *lowering* both the maximum income for non-public assistance families who would be eligible to purchase stamps and the bonus for families already participating, but lowering the cost of the stamps
    C. *raising* the maximum income for non-public assistance families who would be eligible to purchase stamps and lowering the cost of the stamps, but lowering the bonus for families already participating
    D. *lowering* the maximum income for non-public assistance families who would be eligible to purchase stamps and raising the cost of the stamps, but also raising the bonus for families already participating

4. The Federal Revenue Act of 1971 included special benefits for working mothers who have child care expenses in that it provides for deduction of 4._____

    A. specific household and child care expenses for single, divorced, or widowed parents only
    B. specific household and child care expenses for dependents under 15
    C. carfare and other expenses relevant to the mother's employment
    D. allowance for an additional dependent for the person caring for the child

5. A SERIOUS objection raised by those who considered a proposal for revenue sharing by the Federal government to be a major threat to welfare reform is that

   A. states and localities would not have sufficient control over how the money is spent
   B. increased state and local control over expenditures had consistently worked against disadvantaged and minority groups
   C. there are no Federal provisions for enforcement of compliance with regard to discrimination for reason of race, color, or national origin
   D. the state governors would not be able to set their own priorities or monitor violations by local officials

6. Of the following, the SMALLEST number of recipients of public assistance consists of

   A. children under 21
   B. aged adults
   C. employables
   D. adults caring for others

7. Responsibility for quality control studies of public assistance clients' eligibility in the city by means of interviews and analysis of case records has been taken over by the

   A. U.S. Department of Health, Education and Welfare
   B. State Department of Social Services
   C. City Department of Investigation
   D. Bureau of Income Maintenance of the Human Resources Administration

8. The one of the following which is NOT a current method being used by the human services agency in its efforts to reduce welfare costs is

   A. improvement of managerial capability
   B. simplification of procedures
   C. insistence on greater accountability
   D. full investigation of all applicants for assistance

9. The one of the following which would be MOST likely to reduce the tendency of the unemployed poor to migrate to urban centers is

   A. increased federal subsidies to the small farmer
   B. unionization of migrant farm workers
   C. a national guaranteed income maintenance program
   D. an increase in the national minimum wage

10. According to the U.S. Census Bureau Report, economic and educational gains made between 1970 and 1980 by Puerto Ricans living in the city, as compared with Blacks, were

    A. considerably greater
    B. considerably smaller
    C. about the same
    D. slightly greater

11. Of the following, modern child care experts would consider the LEAST desirable setting for treatment of most juvenile offenders while under professional supervision to be

    A. the family's home
    B. a group residence
    C. a foster home
    D. a large institution

12. The state has instituted a program of *work relief,* which requires all Home Relief recipients who are eligible to work but cannot find jobs, to *work off* their welfare checks on non-salaried work projects.
    This approach has met with considerable opposition MAINLY because those who oppose it believe that the recipients

    A. may take away jobs which were formerly performed by paid employees
    B. are unskilled and therefore qualified for an extremely limited number of work assignments
    C. are likely to be resentful and inefficient in carrying out their assignments
    D. will receive no improvement in financial status and no assurance of stable employment so that they can be removed from the welfare rolls

12.____

13. A significant aspect of an amendment to the Social Security Act which became effective recently is that it introduces into the Act a program of

    A. public service jobs
    B. income maintenance
    C. medical assistance to the aged
    D. aid to dependent children

13.____

14. During the past few years, the U.S. Supreme Court has made a series of key rulings that directly affect welfare clients.
    NONE of these rulings has been concerned with

    A. fair hearings
    B. state residence requirements
    C. home inspections
    D. the family assistance plan

14.____

15. A demonstration program for public assistance recipients in the city approved by the U.S. Department of Health, Education, and Welfare which has been the subject of considerable controversy is the

    A. Incentives for Independence Program
    B. Haitian Training Project
    C. Work Incentive Program
    D. Demonstration Work Project

15.____

16. The component of the human services agency which is authorized by the Mayor as the agency to receive community action funds from the Federal government is the

    A. Council Against Poverty
    B. Community Development Agency
    C. Manpower and Career Development Agency
    D. Agency for Child Development

16.____

17. The Equal Employment Opportunity Commission is CORRECTLY described as the

    A. Federal agency which acts on charges of discrimination in employment
    B. state agency which operates employment and specialized placement offices
    C. city agency which develops job opportunities for underemployed persons
    D. city agency which acts on charges of discrimination in employment

17.____

18. The reorganization of the Youth Services Agency emphasized administrative changes that would allow for

    A. expansion of counseling, psychological, and psychiatric services to anti-social youth
    B. greater community responsibility for and participation in the delivery of services to parents
    C. more emphasis on direct services to street youth and fighting gangs
    D. establishment of youth narcotics addiction prevention and treatment programs

18.____

19. The BASIC reason for the establishment of the Agency for Child Development as part of the human services agency was to

    A. provide a single agency to consolidate and administe programs for pre-school-age children
    B. establish a commission to insure maximum parent and community involvement in programs for children
    C. take over the licensing of both public and private programs for pre-school-age children
    D. insure a diversity of programs to meet the needs of a broad spectrum of children

19.____

20. The MAIN functions of the Manpower and Career Development Agency (MCDA) are to

    A. run manpower and recruitment centers under contract with private organizations
    B. train the unskilled, upgrade existing skills, develop job opportunities, and place newly-trained people in jobs
    C. provide remedial education and follow-up for disadvan-taged potential college students, vocational counseling and testing for veterans and ex-addicts
    D. provide job development, interviewing and placement, and manpower research services

20.____

Questions 21-25.

DIRECTIONS: Questions 21 through 25 are to be answered SOLELY on the basis of the following paragraph.

With the generation gap yawning before us, it is well to remember that 20 years ago teenagers produced a larger proportion of unwedlock births than today and that the illegitimacy rate among teenagers is lower than among women in their twenties and thirties. In addition, the illegitimacy rate has risen less among teenagers than among older women.

It is helpful to note the difference between illegitimacy rate and illegitimacy ratio. The ratio is the number of illegitimate babies per 1,000 live births. The rate is the number of illegitimate births per 1,000 unmarried women of childbearing age. The ratio talks about babies; the rate talks about mothers. The ratio is useful for planning services, but worse than useless for considering trends since it depends on the age and marital <u>composition</u> of the population, illegitimacy rate, and the fertility of married women. For example, the ratio among girls under 18 is bound to be high in comparison with older women since few are married mothers. However, the illegitimacy rate is relatively low.

21. Of the following, the MOST suitable title for the above passage would be: 21._____

    A. The Generation Gap
    B. Moral Standards and Teenage Illegitimacy Ratio
    C. A Comparison of Illegitimacy Rate and Illegitimacy Ratio
    D. Causes of High Illegitimacy Rates

22. According to the above passage, which of the following statements is CORRECT? 22._____
    The illegitimacy

    A. rate has fallen among women in their thirties
    B. ratio is the number of illegitimate births per 1,000 unmarried women of childbearing age
    C. ratio is partially dependent on the illegitimacy rate
    D. rate is more useful than the ratio for planning services

23. According to the above passage, of the following age groups, the illegitimacy ratio would 23._____
    be expected to be HIGHEST in comparison with the other groups for the group aged

    A. 17   B. 21   C. 25   D. 29

24. According to the above passage, of the following age groups, the illegitimacy rate would 24._____
    be expected to be LOWEST in comparison with the other groups for the group aged

    A. 17   B. 21   C. 25   D. 29

25. As used in the above passage, the underlined word *composition* means MOST NEARLY 25._____

    A. essay   B. makeup   C. security   D. happiness

Questions 26-30.

DIRECTIONS: Questions 26 through 30 are to be answered SOLELY on the basis of the following paragraph.

In counting the poor, the Social Security Administration has developed two poverty thresholds that <u>designate</u> families as either "poor" or "near poor." The Administration assumed that the poor would spend the same proportion of income on food as the rest of the population but that, obviously, since their income was smaller, their range of selection would be narrower. In the Low Cost Food Plan, the amount <u>allocated to</u> food from the average expenditure was cut to the minimum that the Agriculture Department said could still provide American families with an adequate diet. This Low Cost Food Plan was used to characterize the "near poor" category, and an even lower Economy Food Plan was used to characterize the "poor" category. The Economy Food Plan was based on 70 cents a person for food each day, assuming that all food would be prepared at home. The Agriculture Department estimates that only about 10 percent of persons spending 70 cents or less for food each day actually were able to get a nutritionally adequate diet.

26. Of the following, the MOST suitable title for the above paragraph would be 26._____

    A. The Superiority of the Economy Plan Over the Low Cost Plan
    B. The Need for a Nutritionally Adequate Diet
    C. Food Expenditures of the Poor and the Near Poor
    D. Diet in the United States

27. According to the above paragraph, the Social Security Administration assumed, in setting its poverty levels, that the poor

    A. spend a smaller proportion of income for food than the average non-poor
    B. would not eat in restaurants
    C. as a group includes only those with a nutritionally inadequate diet
    D. spend more money on food than the near poor

28. According to the above paragraph, it would be CORRECT to state that the Low Cost Food Plan

    A. is above the minimum set by the Agriculture Department for a nutritionally adequate diet
    B. gives most people a nutritionally inadequate diet
    C. is lower than the Economy Food Plan
    D. represents the amount spent by the near poor

29. As estimated by the Department of Agriculture, the percentage of people spending 70 cents or less a day for food who did NOT get a nutritionally adequate diet was

    A. 100%   B. 90%   C. 10%   D. 0%

30. As used in the above paragraph, the underlined words *allocated to* mean MOST NEARLY

    A. offered for
    C. wasted on
    B. assigned to
    D. spent on

Questions 31-35.

DIRECTIONS: Questions 31 through 35 are to be answered SOLELY on the basis of the following graphs. Note that the unemployment rate for employables who move into Central City is the same as for the City as a whole.

EMPLOYABLES
IN THOUSANDS

EMPLOYABLES WHO MOVED INTO CENTRAL CITY
1970-1981

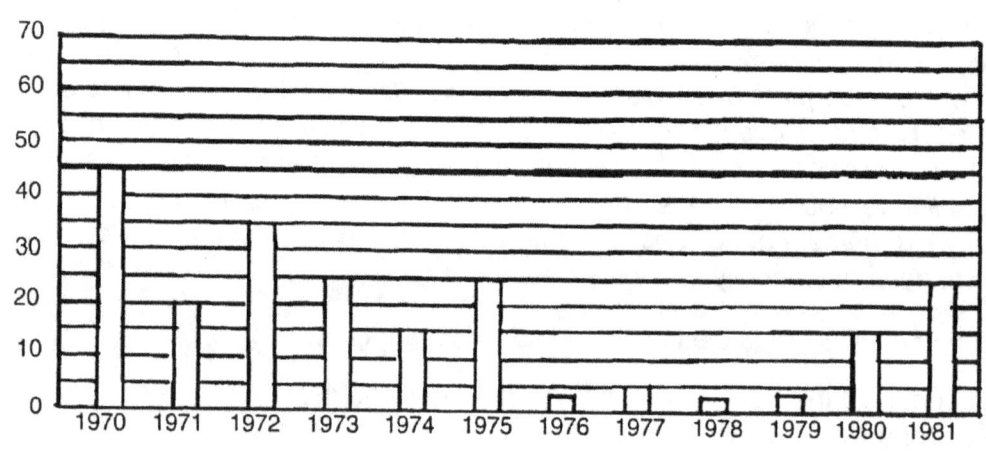

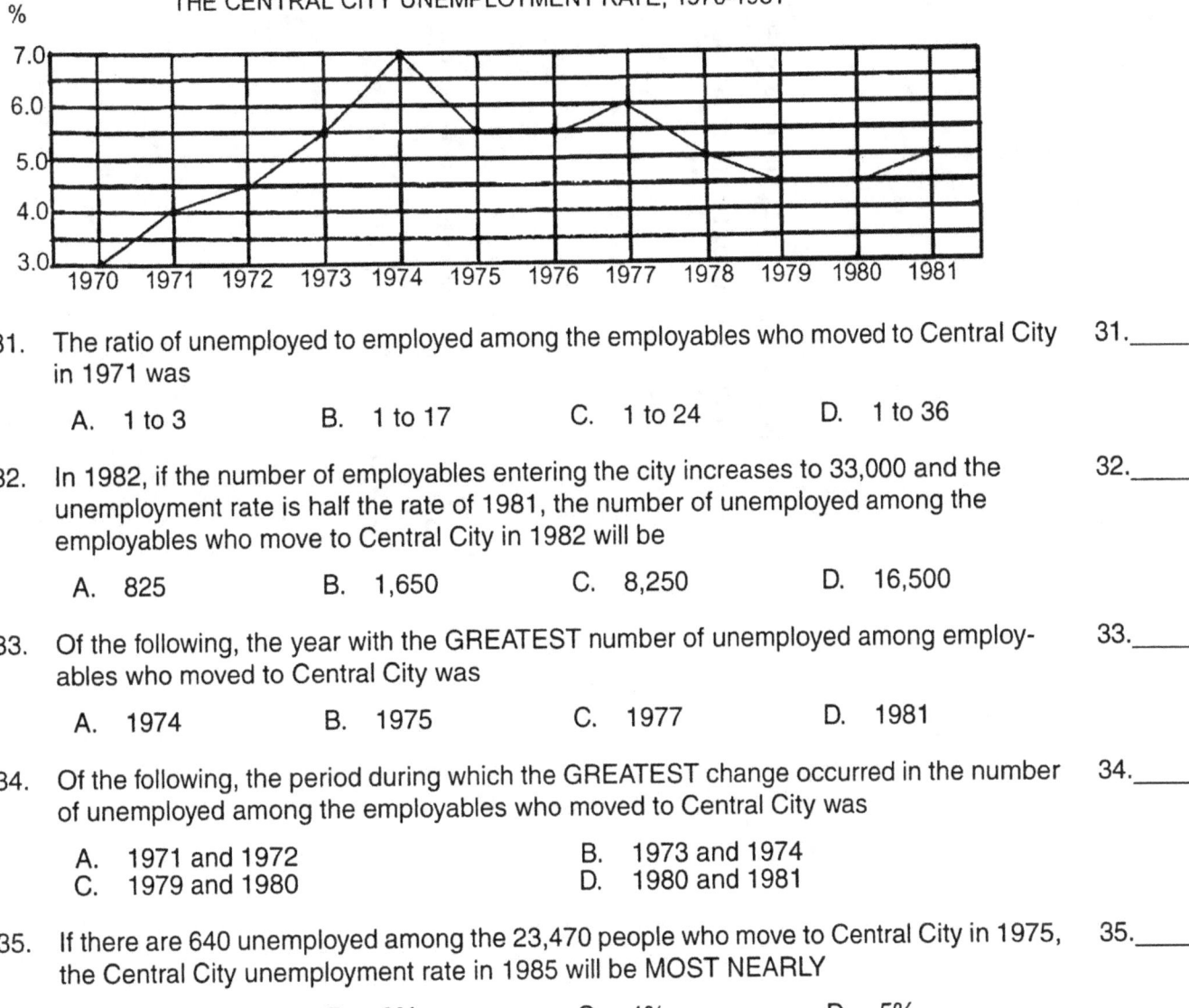

THE CENTRAL CITY UNEMPLOYMENT RATE, 1970-1981

31. The ratio of unemployed to employed among the employables who moved to Central City in 1971 was

    A. 1 to 3   B. 1 to 17   C. 1 to 24   D. 1 to 36

32. In 1982, if the number of employables entering the city increases to 33,000 and the unemployment rate is half the rate of 1981, the number of unemployed among the employables who move to Central City in 1982 will be

    A. 825   B. 1,650   C. 8,250   D. 16,500

33. Of the following, the year with the GREATEST number of unemployed among employables who moved to Central City was

    A. 1974   B. 1975   C. 1977   D. 1981

34. Of the following, the period during which the GREATEST change occurred in the number of unemployed among the employables who moved to Central City was

    A. 1971 and 1972   B. 1973 and 1974
    C. 1979 and 1980   D. 1980 and 1981

35. If there are 640 unemployed among the 23,470 people who move to Central City in 1975, the Central City unemployment rate in 1985 will be MOST NEARLY

    A. 2%   B. 3%   C. 4%   D. 5%

KEY (CORRECT ANSWERS)

1.	B	16.	D
2.	A	17.	A
3.	A	18.	A
4.	B	19.	D
5.	B	20.	B
6.	C	21.	C
7.	B	22.	C
8.	D	23.	A
9.	C	24.	A
10.	B	25.	B
11.	D	26.	C
12.	D	27.	B
13.	A	28.	D
14.	D	29.	B
15.	A	30.	B

31. C
32. A
33. B
34. A
35. B

EXAMINATION SECTION
TEST 1

DIRECTIONS: Each question or incomplete statement is followed by several suggested answers or completions. Select the one that BEST answers the question or completes the statement. *PRINT THE LETTER OF THE CORRECT ANSWER IN THE SPACE AT THE RIGHT.*

1. You find that an applicant for public assistance is hesitant about showing you some required personal material and documents. Your INITIAL reaction to this situation should be to

    A. quietly insist that he give you the required materials
    B. make an exception in his case to avoid making him uncomfortable
    C. suspect that he may be trying to withhold evidence
    D. understand that he is in a stressful situation and may feel ashamed to reveal such information

1.____

2. An applicant has just given you a response which does not seem clear. Of the following, the BEST course of action for you to take in order to check your understanding of the applicant's response is for you to

    A. ask the question again during a subsequent interview with this applicant
    B. repeat the applicant's answer in the applicant.s own words and ask if that is what the applicant meant
    C. later in the interview, repeat the question that led to this response
    D. repeat the question that led to this response, but say it more forcefully

2.____

3. While speaking with applicants for public assistance, you may find that there are times when an applicant will be silent for a short while before answering questions. In order to gather the BEST information from the applicant, the interviewer should *generally* treat these silences by

    A. repeating the same question to make the applicant stop hesitating
    B. rephrasing the question in a way that the applicant can answer it faster
    C. directing an easier question to the applicant so that he can gain confidence in answering
    D. waiting patiently and not pressuring the applicant into quick undeveloped answers

3.____

4. In dealing with members of different ethnic and religious groups among the applicants you interview, you should give

    A. individuals the services to which they are entitled
    B. less service to those you judge to be more advantaged
    C. better service to groups with which you sympathize most
    D. better service to group with political *muscle*

4.____

5. You must be sure that, when interviewing an applicant, you phrase each question carefully. Of the following, the MOST important reason for this is to insure that

    A. the applicant will phrase each of his responses carefully
    B. you use correct grammar
    C. it is clear to the applicant what information you are seeking
    D. you do not word the same question differently for different applicants

5.____

6. When given a form to complete, a client hesitates, tells you that he cannot fill out forms too well, and that he is afraid he will do a poor job. He asks you to do it for him. You are quite sure, however, that he is able to do it himself. In this case, it would be MOST advisable for you to

    A. encourage him to try filling out the application as well as he can
    B. fill out the application for him
    C. explain to him that he must learn to accept responsibility
    D. tell him that, if others can fill out an application, he can too

7. Assume that an applicant for public assistance whom you are interviewing has made a statement that is obviously not true. Of the following, the BEST course of action for you to take at this point in the interview is to

    A. ask the applicant if he is sure about his statement
    B. tell the applicant that his statement is incorrect
    C. question the applicant further to clarify his response
    D. assume that the statement is true

8. Assume that you are conducting an initial interview with an applicant for public assistance. Of the following, the MOST advisable questions for you to ask at the beginning of this interview are questions that

    A. can be answered in one or two sentences
    B. have nothing to do with the subject matter of the interview
    C. are most likely to reveal any hostility on the part of the applicant
    D. the applicant is most likely to be willing and able to answer

9. When interviewing a particularly nervous and upset applicant for public assistance, the one of the following actions which you should take FIRST is to

    A. inform the applicant that, to be helped, he must cooperate
    B. advise the applicant that proof must be provided for statements he makes
    C. assure the applicant that every effort will be made to provide him with whatever assistance he is entitled to
    D. tell the applicant he will have no trouble obtaining public assistance so long as he is truthful

10. Assume that, following normal routine, it is part of your job to prepare a monthly report for your unit head that eventually goes to the Director of your Center. The report contains information on the number of applicants you have interviewed that have been approved for different types of public assistance and the number of applicants you have interviewed that have been turned down. Errors on such reports are *serious* because

    A. you are expected to be able to prove how many applicants you have interviewed each month
    B. accurate statistics are needed for effective management of the department
    C. they may not be discovered before the report is transmitted to the Center Director
    D. they may result in a loss of assistance to the applicants left out of the report

11. During interviews, people give information about themselves in several ways. Which of the following *usually* gives the LEAST amount of information about the person being questioned? His

    A. spoken words
    B. tone of voice
    C. facial expression
    D. body position

12. Suppose an applicant, while being interviewed about his eligibility for public assistance, becomes angered by your questioning and begins to use sharp, uncontrolled language. Which of the following is the BEST way for you to react to him?

    A. Speak in his style to show him that you are neither impressed nor upset by his speech
    B. Interrupt him and tell him that you are not required to listen to this kind of speech
    C. Lower your voice and slow the rate of your speech in an attempt to set an example that will calm him
    D. Let him continue in his way but insist that he answer your questions directly

13. You have been informed that no determination has yet been made on the eligibility of an applicant for public assistance. The decision depends on further checking. His situation, however, is similar to that of many other applicants whose eligibility has been approved. The applicant calls you, quite worried, and asks you whether his application has been accepted. What would be BEST for you to do under these circumstances? Tell him

    A. his application is being checked and you will let him know the final result as soon as possible
    B. that a written request addressed to your supervisor will probably get faster action for his case
    C. not to worry since other applicants with similar backgrounds have already been accepted
    D. since there is no definite information and you are very busy, you will call him back

14. Suppose that you have been talking with an applicant for public assistance. You have the feeling from the latest things the applicant has said that some of his answers to earlier questions were not totally correct. You guess that he might have been afraid or confused earlier but that your conversation has now put him in a more comfortable frame of mind. In order to test the reliability of information received from the earlier questions, the BEST thing for you to do *now* is to ask new questions that

    A. allow the applicant to explain why he deliberately gave false information to you
    B. ask for the same information, although worded differently from the original questions
    C. put pressure on the applicant so that he personally wants to clear up the facts in his earlier answers
    D. indicate to the applicant that you are aware of his deceptiveness

15. Assume that you are a supervisor. While providing you with required information, an applicant for public assistance informs you that she does not know who is the father of her child. Of the following, the MOST advisable action for you to take is to

    A. ask her to explain further
    B. advise her about birth control facilities
    C. express your sympathy for the situation
    D. go on to the next item of information

16. If, in an interview, you wish to determine a client's usual occupation, which one of the following questions is MOST likely to elicit the most useful information?

    A. Did you ever work in a factory?
    B. Do you know how to do office work?
    C. What kind of work do you do?
    D. Where are you working now?

17. Assume that, in the course of the day, you are approached by a clerk from another office who starts questioning you about one of the clients you have just interviewed. The clerk says that she is a relative of the client. According to departmental policy, all matters discussed with clients are to be kept confidential. Of the following, the BEST course of action for you to take in this situation would be to

    A. check to see whether the clerk is really a relative before you make any further decision
    B. explain to the clerk why you cannot divulge the information
    C. tell the clerk that you do not know the answers to her questions
    D. tell the clerk that she can get from the client any information the client wishes to give

18. Which of the following is *usually* the BEST technique for you, as an interviewer, to use to bring an applicant back to subject matter from which the applicant has strayed?

    A. Ask the applicant a question that is related to the subject of the interview
    B. Show the applicant that his response is unrelated to the question
    C. Discreetly remind the applicant that there is a time allotment for the interview
    D. Tell the applicant that you will be happy to discuss the extraneous matters at a future interview

19. Assume that you notice that one of the clerks has accidentally pulled the wrong form to give to her client. Of the following, the BEST way for you to handle this situation would be to tell

    A. the clerk about her error, and precisely describe the problems that will result
    B. the clerk about her error in an understanding and friendly way
    C. the clerk about her error in a humorous way and tell her that no real damage was done
    D. your supervisor that clerks need more training in the use and application of departmental forms

20. Of the following characteristics, the one which would be MOST valuable when helping an angry applicant to understand why he has received less assistance than he believes he is entitled to would be the ability to

    A. state the rules exactly as they apply to the applicant's problem
    B. cite examples of other cases where the results have been similar
    C. remain patient and understanding of the person's feelings
    D. remain completely objective and uninvolved in individual personal problems

21. Reports are usually divided into several sections, some of which are more necessary than others. Of the following, the section which is MOST often necessary to include in a report is a(n)

    A. table of contents
    B. introduction
    C. index
    D. bibliography

22. Suppose you are writing a report on an interview you have just completed with a particularly hostile applicant for public assistance. Which of the following BEST describes what you should include in this report?

    A. What you think caused the applicant.s hostile attitude during the interview
    B. Specific examples of the applicant.s hostile remarks and behavior
    C. The relevant information uncovered during the interview
    D. A recommendation that the applicant.s request be denied because of his hostility

23. When including recommendations in a report to your supervisor, which of the following is MOST important for you to do?

    A. Provide several alternative courses of action for each recommendation
    B. First present the supporting evidence, then the recommendations
    C. First present the recommendations, then the supporting evidence
    D. Make sure the recommendations arise logically out of the information in the report

24. It is often necessary that the writer of a report present facts and sufficient arguments to gain acceptance of the points, conclusions, or recommendations set forth in the report. Of the following, the LEAST advisable step to take in organizing a report, when such argumentation is the important factor, is a(n)

    A. elaborate expression of personal belief
    B. businesslike discussion of the problem as a whole
    C. orderly arrangement of convincing data
    D. reasonable explanation of the primary issues

25. Suppose you receive a phone call from an applicant about a problem which requires that you must look up the information and call her back. Although the applicant had given you her name earlier and you can pronounce the name, you are not sure that you can spell it correctly. Asking the applicant to spell her name is

    A. *good,* because this indicates to the applicant that you intend to obtain the information she requested
    B. *poor,* because she may feel you are making fun of her name
    C. *good,* because you will be sure to get the correct name
    D. *poor,* because she will think you have not been listening to her

KEY (CORRECT ANSWERS)

1. D
2. B
3. D
4. A
5. C

6. A
7. C
8. D
9. C
10. B

11. D
12. C
13. A
14. B
15. D

16. C
17. B
18. A
19. B
20. C

21. B
22. C
23. D
24. A
25. C

TEST 2

DIRECTIONS: Each question or incomplete statement is followed by several suggested answers or completions. Select the one that BEST answers the question or completes the statement. *PRINT THE LETTER OF THE CORRECT ANSWER IN THE SPACE AT THE RIGHT.*

Questions 1-9.

DIRECTIONS: Answer Questions 1 through 9 SOLELY on the basis of the information in the following passage.

The establishment of a procedure whereby the client's rent is paid directly by the Social Service agency has been suggested recently by many people in the Social Service field. It is believed that such a procedure would be advantageous to both the agency and the client. Under the current system, clients often complain that their rent allowances are not for the correct amount. Agencies, in turn, have had to cope with irate landlords who complain that they are not receiving rent checks until much later than their due date.

The proposed new system would involve direct payment of the client's rent by the agency to the landlord. Clients would not receive a monthly rent allowance. Under one possible implementation of such a system, special rent payment offices would be set up in each borough and staffed by Social Service clerical personnel. Each office would handle all work involved in sending out monthly rent payments. Each client would receive monthly notification from the Social Service agency that his rent has been paid. A rent office would be established for every three Social Service centers in each borough. Only in cases where the rental exceeds $700 per month would payment be made and records kept by the Social Service center itself rather than a special rent office. However, clients would continue to make all direct contacts through the Social Service center.

Files in the rent offices would be organized on the basis of client rental. All cases involving monthly rents up to, but not exceeding, $300 would be placed in salmon-colored folders. Cases with rents from $301 to $500 would be placed in buff folders, and those with rents exceeding $500, but less than $700 would be filed in blue folders. If a client's rental changed, he would be required to notify the center as soon as possible so that this information could be brought up-to-date in his folder, and the color of his folder changed if necessary. Included in the information needed, in addition to the amount of rent, are the size of the apartment, the type of heat, and the number of flights of stairs to climb if there is no elevator.

Discussion as to whether the same information should be required of clients residing in city projects was resolved with the decision that the identical system of filing and updating of files should apply to such project tenants. The basic problem that might arise from the institution of such a program is that clients would resent being unable to pay their own rent. However, it is likely that such resentment would be only a temporary reaction to change and would disappear after the new system became standard procedure. It has been suggested that this program first be experimented with on a small scale to determine what problems may arise and how the program can be best implemented.

1. According to the passage, there are a number of complaints about the current system of rent payments. Which of the following is a *complaint* expressed in the passage?

    A. Landlords complain that clients sometimes pay the wrong amount for their rent.
    B. Landlords complain that clients sometimes do not pay their rent on time.

1.____

C. Clients say that the Social Service agency sometimes does not mail the rent out on time.
D. Landlords say that they sometimes fail to receive a check for the rent.

2. Assume that there are 15 Social Service centers in Manhattan. According to the passage, the number of rent offices that should be established in that borough under the new system is

   A. 1   B. 3   C. 5   D. 15

3. According to the passage, a client under the new system would receive

   A. a rent receipt from the landlord indicating that Social Services has paid the rent
   B. nothing since his rent has been paid by Social Services
   C. verification from the landlord that the rent was paid
   D. notices of rent payment from the Social Service agency

4. According to the passage, a case record involving a client whose rent has changed from $310 to $540 per month should be changed from a ____ folder to a ____ folder.

   A. blue; salmon-colored   B. buff; blue
   C. salmon-colored; blue   D. yellow; buff

5. According to the above passage, if a client's rental is lowered because of violations in his building, he would be required to notify the

   A. building department   B. landlord
   C. rent payment office   D. Social Service center

6. Which one of the following kinds of information about a rented apartment is NOT mentioned in the above passage as being necessary to include in the client's folder? The

   A. floor number, if in an apartment house with an elevator
   B. rental, if in a city project apartment
   C. size of the apartment, if in a two-family house
   D. type of heat, if in a city project apartment

7. Assume that the rent payment proposal discussed in the passage is approved and ready for implementation in the city. Which of the following actions is MOST in accordance with the proposal described in the above passage?

   A. Change over completely and quickly to the new system to avoid the confusion of having clients under both systems.
   B. Establish rent payment offices in all of the existing Social Service centers.
   C. Establish one small rent payment office in Manhattan for about six months.
   D. Set up an office in each borough and discontinue issuing rent allowances.

8. According to the passage, it can be *inferred* that the MOST important drawback of the new system would be that once a program is started, clients might feel

   A. they have less independence than they had before
   B. unable to cope with problems that mature people should be able to handle
   C. too far removed from Social Service personnel to successfully adapt to the new requirements
   D. too independent to work with the system

9. The above passage suggests that the proposed rent program be started as a pilot program rather than be instituted immediately throughout the city. Of the following possible reasons for a pilot program, the one which is stated in the passage as the MOST direct reason is that

    A. any change made would then be only on a temporary basis
    B. difficulties should be determined from small-scale implementation
    C. implementation on a wide scale is extremely difficult
    D. many clients might resent the new system

9._____

10. A report is often revised several times before final preparation and distribution in an effort to make certain the report meets the needs of the situation for which it is designed.
    Which of the following is the BEST way for the author to be sure that a report covers the areas he intended?

    A. Obtain a co-worker's opinion.
    B. Compare it with a content checklist.
    C. Test it on a subordinate.
    D. Check his bibliography.

10._____

11. Visual aids used in a report may be placed either in the text material or in the appendix. Deciding where to put a chart, table, or any such aid should depend on the

    A. title of the report
    C. title of the visual aid
    B. purpose of the visual aid
    D. length of the report

11._____

12. In which of the following situations is an oral report PREFERABLE to a written report? When a(n)

    A. recommendation is being made for a future plan of action
    B. department head requests immediate information
    C. long standing policy change is made
    D. analysis of complicated statistical data is involved

12._____

13. When an applicant is approved for public assistance, standard forms with certain information must be filled in.
    The GREATEST advantage of using standard forms in this situation rather than writing the report as you see fit is that

    A. the report can be acted on quickly
    B. the report can be written without directions from a supervisor
    C. needed information is less likely to be left out of the report
    D. information that is written up this way is more likely to be verified

13._____

14. In some types of reports, visual aids add interest, meaning, and support. They also provide an essential means of effectively communicating the message of the report.
    Of the following, the selection of the suitable visual aids to use with a report is LEAST dependent on the

    A. nature and scope of the report
    C. aids used in other reports
    B. way in which the aid is to be used
    D. prospective readers of the report

14._____

15. He wanted to ASCERTAIN the facts before arriving at a conclusion. The word ASCERTAIN means *most nearly*

    A. disprove B. determine C. convert D. provide

16. Did the supervisor ASSENT to her request for annual leave? The word ASSENT means *most nearly*

    A. allude B. protest C. agree D. refer

17. The new worker was fearful that the others would REBUFF her. The word REBUFF means *most nearly*

    A. ignore B. forget C. copy D. snub

18. The supervisor of that office does not CONDONE lateness. The word CONDONE means *most nearly*

    A. mind B. excuse C. punish D. remember

19. Each employee was instructed to be as CONCISE as possible when preparing a report. The word CONCISE means *most nearly*

    A. exact B. sincere C. flexible D. brief

20. Despite many requests for them, there was a SCANT supply of new blotters. The word SCANT means *most nearly*

    A. adequate B. abundant
    C. insufficient D. expensive

21. Did they REPLENISH the supply of forms in the cabinet? The word REPLENISH means *most nearly*

    A. straighten up B. refill
    C. sort out D. use

22. Employees may become bored if they are assigned DIVERSE duties. The word DIVERSE means *most nearly*

    A. interesting B. different
    C. challenging D. enjoyable

23. During the probation period, the worker proved to be INEPT. The word INEPT means *most nearly*

    A. incompetent B. insubordinate
    C. satisfactory D. uncooperative

24. The PUTATIVE father was not living with the family. The word PUTATIVE means *most nearly*

    A. reputed B. unemployed
    C. concerned D. indifferent

25. The adopted child researched various documents of VITAL STATISTICS in an effort to discover the names of his natural parents. The words VITAL STATISTICS means *most nearly* statistics relating to

    A. human life B. hospitals
    C. important facts D. health and welfare

KEY (CORRECT ANSWERS)

1.	B	11.	B
2.	C	12.	B
3.	D	13.	C
4.	B	14.	C
5.	D	15.	B
6.	A	16.	C
7.	C	17.	D
8.	A	18.	B
9.	B	19.	D
10.	B	20.	C

21. B
22. B
23. A
24. A
25. A

EXAMINATION SECTION
TEST 1

DIRECTIONS: Each question or incomplete statement is followed by several suggested answers or completions. Select the one that BEST answers the question or completes the statement. *PRINT THE LETTER OF THE CORRECT ANSWER IN THE SPACE AT THE RIGHT.*

Questions 1-4.

DIRECTIONS: Questions 1 through 4 are to be answered SOLELY on the basis of the information in the paragraphs below.

Some authorities have questioned whether the term "culture of poverty" should be used since "culture" means a design for living which is passed down from generation to generation. The culture of poverty is, however, a very useful concept if it is used with care, with recognition that poverty is a subculture, and with avoidance of the "cookie-cutter" approach. With regard to the individual, the cookie-cutter view assumes that all individuals in a culture turn out exactly alike, as if they were so many cookies. It overlooks the fact that, at least in our urban society, every individual is a member of more than one subculture; and which subculture most strongly influences his response in a given situation depends on the interaction of a great many factors, including his individual makeup and history, the specifics of the various subcultures to which he belongs, and the specifics of the given situation. It is always important to avoid the cookie-cutter view of culture, with regard to the individual and to the culture or subculture involved.

With regard to the culture as a whole, the cookie-cutter concept again assumes homogeneity and consistency. It forgets that within any one culture or subculture there are conflicts and contradictions, and that at any given moment an individual may have to choose, consciously, between conflicting values or patterns. Also, most individuals, in varying degrees, have a dual set of values - those by which they live and those they cherish as best. This point has been made and documented repeatedly about the culture of poverty.

1. The *cookie-cutter* approach assumes that

   A. members of the same *culture* are all alike
   B. *culture* stays the same from generation to generation
   C. the term *culture* should not be applied to groups who are poor
   D. there are value conflicts within most cultures

1._____

2. According to the passage, every person in our cities

   A. is involved in the conflicts of urban culture
   B. recognizes that poverty is a subculture
   C. lives by those values to which he is exposed
   D. belongs to more than one subculture

2._____

3. The above passage emphasizes that a culture is likely to contain within it

   A. one dominant set of values
   B. a number of contradictions

3._____

C. one subculture to which everyone belongs
D. members who are exactly alike

4. According to the above passage, individuals are sometimes forced to choose between

A. cultures
B. subcultures
C. different sets of values
D. a new culture and an old culture

Questions 5-8.

DIRECTIONS: Questions 5 through 8 are to be answered SOLELY on the basis of the following passage.

There are approximately 33 million poor people in the United States; 14.3 million of them are children, 5.3 million are old people, and the remainder are in other categories. Altogether, 6.5 million families live in poverty because the heads of the households cannot works they are either too old or too sick or too severely handicapped, or they are widowed or deserted mothers of young children. There are the working poor, the low-paid workers, the workers in seasonal industries, and soldiers with no additional income who are heads of families. There are the underemployed: those who would like full-time jobs but cannot find them, those employees who would like year-round work but lack the opportunity, and those who are employed below their level of training. There are the non-working poor: the older men and women With small retirement incomes and those with no income, the disabled, the physically and mentally handicapped, and the chronically sick.

5. According to the above passage, APPROXIMATELY what percent of the poor people in the United States are children?

A. 33   B. 16   C. 20   D. 44

6. According to the above passage, people who work in seasonal industries are LIKELY to be classified as

A. working poor
B. underemployed
C. non-working poor
D. low-paid workers

7. According to the above passage, the category of non-working poor includes people who

A. receive unemployment insurance
B. cannot find full-time work
C. are disabled or mentally handicapped
D. are soldiers with wives and children

8. According to the above passage, among the underemployed are those who

A. can find only part-time work
B. are looking for their first jobs
C. are inadequately trained
D. depend on insufficient retirement incomes

Questions 9-18.

DIRECTIONS: Questions 9 through 18 are to be answered SOLELY on the basis of the information given in the following charts.

CHILD CARE SERVICES 1997-2001

CHILDREN IN FOSTER HOMES AND VOLUNTARY INSTITUTIONS, BY TYPE OF CARE, IN NEW YORK CITY AND UPSTATE* NEW YORK

Year End	FOSTER FAMILY HOMES			Total in Foster Family Homes	Total in Voluntary Institutions	Total in Other	Total Number of Children
	Boarding Homes	Adoptive or Free Homes	Wage, Work or Self-Supportine				
New York City							
1997	12,389	1,773	33	14,195	7,187	1,128	22,510
1998	13,271	1,953	42	15,266	7,227	1,237	23,730
1999	14,012	2,134	32	16,178	7,087	1,372	24,637
2000	14,558	2,137	29	16,724	6,717	1,437	24,778
2001	14,759	2,241	37	17,037	6,777	1,455	25,264
Upstate							
1997	14,801	2,902	90	17,793	3,012	241	21,046
1998	15,227	2,943	175	18,345	3,067	291	21,703
1999	16,042	3,261	64	19,367	2,940	273	22,580
2000	16,166	3,445	60	19,671	2,986	362	23,121
2001	16,357	3,606	55	20,018	3,024	485	23,527

*Upstate is defined as all of New York State, excluding New York City.

NUMBER OF CHILDREN, BY AGE, UNDER FOSTER FAMILY CARE IN NEW YORK CITY IN 2001

Borough	Children's Ages					Total All Ages
	One Year or Younger	Two Years	Three Years	Four Years	Over Four Years	
Manhattan	1,054	1,170	1,060	1,325	445	5,070
Bronx	842	1,196	1,156	1,220	484	4,882
Brooklyn	707	935	470	970	361	?
Queens	460	555	305	793	305	2,418
Richmond	270	505	160	173	112	1.224
Total All Boroughs	3,337	4,361	3,151	4,481	?	17,037

9. According to the table, Child Care Services, 1997-2001, the number of children in New York City boarding homes was AT LEAST twice the number of children in New York City voluntary institutions in _____ of the five years.

    A. *only* one   B. *only* two   C. *only* three   D. all

9.____

10. If the number of children cared for in voluntary institutions in New York State increases from 2001 to 2002 by exactly the same number as from 2000 to 2001, then the 2002 year-end total of children in voluntary institutions in New York State will be

   A. 3,062   B. 6,837   C. 7,494   D. 9,899

11. If the total number of children under child care services in New York City in 1997 was 25% more than in 1996, then the 1996 New York City total was MOST NEARLY

   A. 11,356   B. 11,647   C. 16,883   D. 18,008

12. From 1997 through 2001, the New York State five-year average of children in Child Care Services classified as *other* is MOST NEARLY

   A. 330   B. 728   C. 1,326   D. 1,656

13. Of all the children under foster family care in the Bronx in 2001, the percentage who were one year of age or younger is MOST NEARLY

   A. 16%   B. 17%   C. 18%   D. 19%

14. Suppose that in New York State the *wage, work, or self-supporting* type of foster family care is given only to children between the ages of 14 and 18, and that, of the children in *adoptive or free home* foster care in each of the five years listed, only one percent each year are between the ages of 14 and 18.
    The TOTAL number of 14 to 18-year-olds under foster family care in Upstate New York exceeded 95 in _____ of the five years.

   A. each   B. four   C. three   D. two

15. The average number of two-year-olds under foster family care in New York City's boroughs in 2001 is MOST NEARLY

   A. 872   B. 874   C. 875   D. 882

16. The difference between the total number of children of all ages under foster family care in Brooklyn in 2001 and the total number under foster care in Richmond that year is

   A. 1,224   B. 2,219   C. 3,443   D. 4,667

17. Suppose that by the end of 2002 the number of children one year or younger under foster family care in Queens will be twice the 2001 total, while the number of two-year-olds will be four-fifths the 2001 total.
    The 2002 total of children two years or younger under foster family care in Queens will be

   A. 2,418   B. 1,624   C. 1,364   D. 1,015

18. The TOTAL number of children over four years of age under foster care in New York City in 2001 was

   A. 1,607   B. 1,697   C. 1,707   D. 1,797

19. At the start of a year, a family was receiving a public assistance grant of $191 twice a month, on the 1st and 15th of each month. On March 1, their rent allowance was decreased from $75 to $71 a month since they had moved to a smaller apartment. On August 1, their semimonthly food allowance, which had been $40.20, was raised by 10%. In that year, the TOTAL amount of money disbursed to this family was

   A. $2,272.10 B. $3,290.70
   C. $4,544.20 D. $4,584.20

20. It is discovered that a client has received double public assistance for 2 months by having been enrolled at two service centers of the Department of Social Services. The client should have received $84.00 twice a month instead of the double amount. He now agrees to repay the money by equal deductions from his public assistance check over a period of 12 months.
    What will the amount of his NEXT check be?

   A. $56 B. $70 C. $77 D. $80

21. Suppose a study is being made of the composition of 3,550 families receiving public assistance. Of the first 1,050 families reviewed, 18% had four or more children.
    If, in the remaining number of families, the percentage with four or more children is half as high as the percentage in the group already reviewed, then the percentage of families with four or more children in the entire group of families is MOST NEARLY

   A. 12 B. 14 C. 16 D. 27

22. Suppose that food prices have risen 13%, and an increase of the same amount has been granted in the food allotment given to people receiving public assistance.
    If a family has been receiving $405 a month, 35% of which is allotted for food, then the TOTAL amount of public assistance this family receives per month will be changed to

   A. $402.71 B. $420.03 C. $423.43 D. $449.71

23. Assume that the food allowance is to be raised 5% in August but will be retroactive for four months to April. The retroactive allowance is to be divided into equal sections and added to the public assistance checks for August, September, October, November, and December.
    A family which has been receiving $420 monthly, 40% of which was allotted for food, will receive what size check in August?

   A. $426.72 B. $428.40 C. $430.50 D. $435.12

24. A blind client, who receives $105 public assistance twice a month, inherits 14 shares of stock worth $90 each. The client is required to sell the stock and spend his inheritance before receiving more public assistance.
    Using his public assistance allowance as a guide, how many months are his new assets expected to last?

   A. 6 B. 7 C. 8 D. 12

25. The Department of Social Services has 16 service centers in Manhattan. These centers may be divided into those which are downtown (south of Central Park) and those which are uptown. Two of the centers are special service centers and are downtown, while the remainder of the centers are general service centers. There is a total of 7 service centers downtown.

    The percentage of the general service centers which are uptown is MOST NEARLY

    A. 56   B. 64   C. 69   D. 79

    25. ___

KEY (CORRECT ANSWERS)

1. A
2. D
3. B
4. C
5. D

6. A
7. C
8. A
9. B
10. D

11. D
12. D
13. B
14. C
15. A

16. B
17. C
18. C
19. D
20. B

21. A
22. C
23. D
24. A
25. B

TEST 2

DIRECTIONS: Each question or incomplete statement is followed by several suggested answers or completions. Select the one that BEST answers the question or completes the statement. *PRINT THE LETTER OF THE CORRECT ANSWER IN THE SPACE AT THE RIGHT.*

1. On January 1, a family was receiving supplementary monthly public assistance of $56 for food, $48 for rent, and $28 for other necessities. In the spring, their rent rose by 10%, and their rent allowance was adjusted accordingly.
   In the summer, due to the death of a family member, their allotments for food and other necessities were reduced by 1/7.
   Their monthly allowance check in the fall should be

   A. $124.80   B. $128.80   C. $132.80   D. $136.80   1.____

2. Twice a month, a certain family receives a $170 general allowance for rent, food, and clothing expenses. In addition, the family receives a specific supplementary allotment for utilities of $192 a year, which is added to their semi-monthly check.
   If the general allowance alone is reduced by 5%, what will be the TOTAL amount of their next semi-monthly check?

   A. $161.50   B. $169.50   C. $170.00   D. $177.50   2.____

3. If each clerk in a certain unit sees an average of 9 clients in a 7-hour day and there are 15 clerks in the unit, APPROXIMATELY how many clients will be seen in a 35-hour week?   3.____

   A. 315   B. 405   C. 675   D. 945

4. The program providing federal welfare aid to the state and its cities is intended to expand services to public assistance recipients.
   All of the following services are included in the program EXCEPT   4.____

   A. homemaker/housekeeper services
   B. mental health clinics
   C. abortion clinics
   D. narcotic addiction control services

5. The Department of Consumer Affairs is NOT concerned with regulation of   5.____

   A. prices   B. product service guarantees
   C. welfare fraud   D. product misrepresentation

6. A plan to control the loss of welfare monies would likely contain all of the following EXCEPT   6.____

   A. identification cards with photographs of the welfare client
   B. individual cash payments to each member of a family
   C. computerized processing of welfare money records
   D. face-to-face interviews with the welfare clients

27

7. The state law currently allows a woman to obtain an abortion

    A. only if it is intended to save her life
    B. if three doctors confirm the need for such treatment
    C. if it does not conflict with her religious beliefs
    D. upon her request, up to the 24th week of pregnancy

7.____

8. Under the city's public assistance program, allocations for payment of a client's rent and security deposits are given in check form directly to the welfare recipient and not to the landlord.
   This practice is used in the city MAINLY as an effort to

    A. increase the client's responsibility for his own affairs
    B. curb the rent overcharges made by most landlords in the city
    C. control the number of welfare recipients housed in public housing projects
    D. limit the number of checks issued to each welfare family

8.____

9. The city plans to save 100 million dollars a year in public assistance costs.
   To achieve this goal, the Human Resources Administration and the Department of Social Services may take any of the following steps EXCEPT

    A. tightening controls on public assistance eligibility requirements
    B. intensifying the investigations of relief frauds
    C. freezing the salaries of all agency employees for a one-year period
    D. cutting the services extended to public assistance clients

9.____

10. Recently, the state instituted a work relief program under which employable recipients of Home Relief and Aid to Dependent Children are given jobs to help work off their relief grants.
    Under the present work relief program, program recipients are NOT required to

    A. report to state employment offices every two weeks to pick up their welfare checks
    B. live within a two-mile radius of the job site to which they are referred
    C. respond to offers of part-time jobs in public agencies
    D. take job training courses offered through the State Employment Service

10.____

11. Of the following, the MOST inclusive program designed to help selected cities to substantially improve social, physical, and economic conditions in specially selected slum neighborhoods is known as the

    A. Model Cities Program
    B. Neighborhood Youth Corps Program
    C. Urban Renewal Program
    D. Emergency Employment Act

11.____

12. The crusade against environmental hazards in the United States is concentrated in urban areas MOSTLY on the problems of

    A. air pollution, sewage treatment, and noise
    B. garbage collection
    C. automobile exhaust fumes and street cleanliness
    D. recycling, reconstitution, and open space

12.____

Questions 13-16.

DIRECTIONS: Questions 13 through 16 are to be answered SOLELY on the basis of the information in the following passage.

City social work agencies and the police have been meeting at City Hall to coordinate efforts to defuse the tensions among teenage groups that they fear could flare into warfare once summer vacations begin. Police intelligence units, with the help of the District Attorneys' offices, are gathering information to identify gangs and their territories. A list of 3,000 gang members has already been assembled, and 110 gangs have been identified. Social workers from various agencies like the Department of Social Services, Neighborhood youth Corps, and the Youth Board are out every day developing liaison with groups of juveniles through meetings at schools and recreation centers. Many street workers spend their days seeking to ease the intergang hostility, tracing potentially incendiary rumors, and trying to channel willing gang members into participation in established summer programs. The city's Youth Services Agency plans to spend a million dollars for special summer programs in ten main city areas where gang activity is most firmly entrenched. Five of the "gang neighborhoods" are clustered in an area forming most of southeastern Bronx, and it is here that most of the 110 identified gangs have formed. Special Youth Services programs will also be directed toward the Rockaway section of Queens, Chinatown, Washington Heights, and two neighborhoods in northern Staten Island noted for a lot of motorcycle gang activity. Some of these programs will emphasize sports and recreation, others vocational guidance or neighborhood improvement, but each program will be aimed at benefiting all youngsters in the area. Although none of the money will be spent specifically on gang members, the Youth Services Agency is consulting gang leaders, along with other teenagers, on the projects they would like developed in their area.

13. The above passage states that one of the steps taken by street workers in trying to defuse the tensions among teenage gangs is that of

    A. conducting summer school sessions that will benefit all neighborhood youth
    B. monitoring neighborhood sports competitions between rival gangs
    C. developing liaison with community school boards and parent associations
    D. tracing rumors that could intensify intergang hostilities

14. Based on the information given in the above passage on gangs and New York City's gang members, it is CORRECT to state that

    A. there are no teenage gangs located in Brooklyn
    B. most of the gangs identified by the police are concentrated in one borough
    C. there is a total of 110 gangs in New York City
    D. only a small percentage of gangs in New York City is in Queens

15. According to the above passage, one IMPORTANT aspect of the program is that

    A. youth gang leaders and other teenagers are involved in the planning
    B. money will be given directly to gang members for use on their projects
    C. only gang members will be allowed to participate in the programs
    D. the parents of gang members will act as youth leaders

16. Various city agencies are cooperating in the attempt to keep the city's youth *cool* during the summer school vacation period.
    The above passage does NOT specifically indicate participation in this project by the

    A. Police Department
    B. District Attorney's Office
    C. Board of Education
    D. Department of Social Services

Questions 17-19.

DIRECTIONS: Questions 17 through 19 are to be answered SOLELY on the basis of the information in the following passage.

It is important that interviewers understand to some degree the manner in which stereotyped thinking operates. Stereotypes are commonly held, but predominantly false, preconceptions about the appearance and traits of individuals of different racial, religious, ethnic, and subcultural groups. Distinct traits, physical and mental, are associated with each group, and membership in a particular group is enough, in the mind of a person holding the stereotype, to assure that these traits will be perceived in individuals who are members of that group. Conversely, possession of the particular stereotyped trait by an individual usually indicates to the holder of the stereotype that the individual is a group member. Linked to the formation of stereotypes is the fact that mental traits, either positive or negative, such as honesty, laziness, avariciousness, and other characteristics are associated with particular stereotypes. Either kind of stereotype, if held by an interviewer, can seriously damage the results of an interview. In general, stereotypes can be particularly dangerous when they are part of the belief patterns of administrators, interviewers, and supervisors, who are in a position to affect the lives of others and to stimulate or retard the development of human potential. The holding of a stereotype by an interviewer, for example, diverts his attention from significant essential facts and information upon which really valid assessments may be made. Unfortunately, it is the rare interviewer who is completely conscious of the real basis upon which he is making his evaluation of the people he is interviewing. The specific reasons given by an interviewer for a negative evaluation, even though apparently logical and based upon what, in the mind of the interviewer, are very good reasons, may not be the truly motivating factors. This is why the careful selection and training of interviewers is such an important responsibility of an agency which is attempting to help a great diversity of human beings.

17. Of the following, the BEST title for the above paragraph is

    A. POSITIVE AND NEGATIVE EFFECTS OF STEREOTYPED THINKING
    B. THE RELATIONSHIP OF STEREOTYPES TO INTERVIEWING
    C. AN AGENCY'S RESPONSIBILITY IN INTERVIEWING
    D. THE IMPACT OF STEREOTYPED THINKING ON PROFESSIONAL FUNCTIONS

18. According to the above passage, MOST interviewers

    A. compensate for stereotyped beliefs to avoid negatively affecting the results of their interviews
    B. are influenced by stereotypes they hold, but put greater stress on factual information developed during the interview
    C. are seldom aware of their real motives when evaluating interviewees
    D. give logical and good reasons for negative evaluations of interviewees

19. According to the above passage, which of the following is NOT a characteristic of stereo-   19.____
    types?

    A. Stereotypes influence estimates of personality traits of people.
    B. Positive stereotypes can damage the results of an interview.
    C. Physical traits associated with stereotypes seldom really exist.
    D. Stereotypes sometimes are a basis upon which valid personality assessments can be made.

Questions 20-25.

DIRECTIONS: Questions 20 through 25 are to be answered SOLELY on the basis of the information in the following passage.

   The quality of the voice of a worker is an important factor in conveying to clients and co-workers his attitude and, to some degree, his character. The human voice, when not consciously disguised, may reflect a person's mood, temper, and personality. It has been shown in several experiments that certain character traits can be assessed with better than chance accuracy through listening to the voice of an unknown person who cannot be seen.

   Since one of the objectives of the worker is to put clients at ease and to present an encouraging and comfortable atmosphere, a harsh, shrill, or loud voice could have a negative effect. A client who displays emotions of anger or resentment would probably be provoked even further by a caustic tone. In a face-to-face situation, an unpleasant voice may be compensated for to some degree by a concerned and kind facial expression. However, when one speaks on the telephone, the expression on one's face cannot be seen by the listener. A supervising clerk who wishes to represent himself effectively to clients should try to eliminate as many faults as possible in striving to develop desirable voice qualities.

20. If a worker uses a sarcastic tone while interviewing a resentful client, the client, accord-   20.____
    ing to the above passage, would MOST likely

    A. avoid the face-to-face situation
    B. be ashamed of his behavior
    C. become more resentful
    D. be provoked to violence

21. According to the above passage, experiments comparing voice and character traits have   21.____
    demonstrated that

    A. prospects for improving an unpleasant voice through training are better than chance
    B. the voice can be altered to project many different psychological characteristics
    C. the quality of the human voice reveals more about the speaker than his words do
    D. the speaker's voice tells the hearer something about the speaker's personality

22. Which of the following, according to the above passage, is a person's voice MOST likely   22.____
    to reveal?
    His

    A. prejudices   B. intelligence
    C. social awareness   D. temperament

23. It may be MOST reasonably concluded from the above passage that an interested and sympathetic expression on the face of a worker   23.____

    A. may induce a client to feel certain he will receive welfare benefits
    B. will eliminate the need for pleasant vocal qualities in the interviewer
    C. may help to make up for an unpleasant voice in the interviewer
    D. is desirable as the interviewer speaks on the telephone to a client

24. Of the following, the MOST reasonable implication of the above paragraph is that a worker should, when speaking to a client, control and use his voice to   24.____

    A. simulate a feeling of interest in the problems of the client
    B. express his emotions directly and adequately
    C. help produce in the client a sense of comfort and security
    D. reflect his own true personality

25. It may be concluded from the passage that the PARTICULAR reason for a worker to pay special attention to modulating her voice when talking on the phone to a client is that, during a telephone conversation,   25.____

    A. there is a necessity to compensate for the way in which a telephone distorts the voice
    B. the voice of the worker is a reflection of her mood and character
    C. the client can react only on the basis of the voice and words she hears
    D. the client may have difficulty getting a clear understanding over the telephone

KEY (CORRECT ANSWERS)

1. A   11. A
2. B   12. A
3. C   13. D
4. C   14. B
5. C   15. A

6. B   16. C
7. D   17. B
8. A   18. C
9. C   19. D
10. B   20. C

21. D
22. D
23. C
24. C
25. C

EXAMINATION SECTION
TEST 1

DIRECTIONS: Each question or incomplete statement is followed by several suggested answers or completions. Select the one that BEST answers the question or completes the statement. *PRINT THE LETTER OF THE CORRECT ANSWER IN THE SPACE AT THE RIGHT.*

1. The applicant you are interviewing is a man in his late forties who has recently lost his job and has a family of eight to support. He is very upset and tells you he does not know where he will get the money to purchase food for the family and pay the rent. He does not know what he will do if he is found not eligible for public assistance. He asks you whether you think he will be eligible. You feel the applicant has a good chance, and you think he should receive financial assistance, but you are not completely certain that he is eligible for public assistance under departmental policy.
Of the following, the BEST action for you to take is to

   A. reassure the applicant and tell him you are sure everything will be all right because there is no sense in worrying him before you know for certain that he is not eligible
   B. tell the applicant that as far as you are concerned he should receive public assistance but that you are not certain the department will go along with your recommendation
   C. tell the applicant that you are not sure that he will be found eligible for public assistance
   D. adopt a cool manner and tell the applicant that he must behave like an adult and not allow himself to become emotional about the situation

1.____

2. When conducting an interview with a client receiving public assistance, it would be LEAST important for you to try to

   A. understand the reasons for the client's statements
   B. conduct the interview on the client's intellectual level
   C. imitate the client's speech as much as possible
   D. impress the client with the agency's concern for his welfare

2.____

Questions 3-6.

DIRECTIONS: Questions 3 through 6 are to be answered SOLELY on basis of the following case history of the Foster family.

2 (#1)

FOSTER CASE HISTORY

Form W-341-C
Rev. 3/1/03
600M-804077-S-200 (93)-245

Date: Jan. 25, 2015
Case Name: Foster
Case No. : ADC-3415968

Family Composition: Ann Foster, b. 7.23.77
Gerry b. 1.7.02
Susan b. 4.1.04
John b. 5.3.07
Joan b. 10.14.10

Mrs. Foster was widowed in June 2011 when her husband was killed in a car accident. Since that time, the family has received public assistance. Mrs. Foster has been referred for housekeeping service by the Social Service Department of Lincoln Hospital, where she is being treated in the neurology clinic. Her primary diagnosis is multiple sclerosis. The hospital reports that she is going through a period of deterioration characterized by an unsteady gait, and weakness and tremor in the limbs. At this time, her capacity to manage a household and four children is severely limited. She feels quite overwhelmed and is unable to function adequately in taking care of her home.

In addition to the medical reasons, it is advisable that a housekeeper be placed in the home as part of a total plan to avoid further family breakdown and deterioration. This deterioration is reflected by all family members. Mrs. Foster is severely depressed and is unable to meet the needs of her children, who have a variety of problems. Joan, the youngest, is not speaking, is hyperactive, and in general is not developing normally for a child her age. John is showing learning problems in school and has poor articulation. Susan was not promoted last year and is a behavior problem at home. Gerry, the oldest, is deformed due to a fire at age two. It is clear that Mrs. Foster cannot control or properly discipline her children, but even more important is the fact that she is unable to offer them the encouragement and guidance they require.

It is hoped that providing housekeeping service will relieve Mrs. Foster of the basic household chores so that she will be less frustrated and better able to provide the love and guidance needed by her children.

3. The age of the child who is described as not developing normally, hyperactive, and not speaking is

    A. 4   B. 7   C. 10   D. 13

4. Which of the following CANNOT be verified on the basis of the Foster Case History above?

    A. William Foster was Ann Foster's husband.
    B. Mrs. Foster has been seen in the neurology clinic at Lincoln Hospital.
    C. John Foster has trouble with his speech.
    D. The Foster family has received public assistance since June 2011.

5. The form on which the information about the Foster family is presented is known as

    A. Family Composition Form   B. Form Rev. 3/1/03
    C. Form W-341-C   D. ADC-3415968

6. According to the above case history, housekeeping service is being requested PRIMA- 6.____
   RILY because

   A. no one in the family can perform the household chores
   B. Mrs. Foster suffers from multiple sclerosis and requires assistance with the household chores
   C. the children are exhibiting behavior problems resulti from the mother's illness
   D. the children have no father

7. You notice that an applicant whom you rejected for public assistance is back at the center 7.____
   the following morning and is waiting to be interviewed by another worker in your group.
   Of the following, the BEST approach for you to take is to

   A. inform the worker, before she interviews the applicant that you had interviewed and rejected him the previous day
   B. not inform the worker about the situation and let her make her own decision
   C. approach the applicant and tell him he was rejected for good reason and will have to leave the center immediately
   D. ask the special officer at the center to remove the applicant

8. You have just finished interviewing an applicant who has a violent temper and has dis- 8.____
   played a great amount of hostility toward you during the interview. You find he is ineligible
   for public assistance. Departmental policy is that all applicants are notified by mail in a
   day or so of their acceptance or rejection for public assistance. However, you also have
   the option, if you think it is desirable, of notifying the applicant at the interview.
   Of the following, the BEST action for you to take in this case is to

   A. tell the applicant of his rejection during the interview
   B. have the applicant notified of the results of the interview by mail only
   C. ask your supervisor to inform the applicant of his rejection
   D. inform the applicant of the results of the interview, with a special patrolman at your side

9. You are interviewing a client who speaks English poorly and whose native language is 9.____
   Spanish. Your knowledge of Spanish is very limited.
   Of the following, the FIRST action it would be best for you to take is to

   A. try to locate a worker at the center who speaks Spanish
   B. write our your questions because it is easier for people to understand a new language when it is written rather than when it is spoken
   C. do the best you can, using hand gestures to make yourself understood
   D. tell the client to return with a friend or relative who speaks English

10. During an interview with a client of another race, he accuses you of racial prejudice and 10.____
    asks for an interviewer of his own race.
    Of the following, which is the BEST way to handle the situation?

    A. In a friendly manner, tell the client that eligibility is based on the regulations and the facts, not on prejudice, and ask him to continue with the interview.
    B. Explain to your supervisor that you cannot deal with someone who accuses you of prejudice, and ask your supervisor to assign the client someone of his own race.
    C. Assure the client that you will lean over backwards to treat his application favorably.

D. Tell the client that some of your friends are of his race and that you could therefore not possibly be prejudiced.

Questions 11-15.

DIRECTIONS: In order to answer Questions 11 through 15, assume that you have been asked to write a short report on the basis of the information contained in the following passage about the granting of emergency funds to the Smith family.

Mr. and Mrs. Smith, who have been receiving public assistance for the last six months, arrive at the center the morning of August 2, totally upset and anxious because they and their family have been burned out of their apartment the night before. The fire seems to have been of suspicious origin because at the time it broke out witnesses spotted two neighborhood teenagers running away from the scene. The policemen, who arrived at the scene shortly after the firemen, took down the pertinent information about the alleged arsonists.

The Smiths have spent the night with friends but now request emergency housing and emergency funds for themselves and their four children to purchase food and to replace the clothing which was destroyed by the fire. The burned-out apartment had consisted of 5 rooms and a bath, and the Smiths are now worried that they will be forced to accept smaller accommodations. Furthermore, since Mrs. Smith suffers from a heart murmur, she is worried that their new living quarters will necessitate her climbing too many stairs. Her previous apartment was a one-flight walk-up, which was acceptable.

As the worker in charge, you have studied the case, determined the amount of the emergency grant, made temporary arrangements for the Smiths to stay at a hotel, and reassured Mrs. Smith that everything possible will be done to find them an apartment which will meet with their approval.

11. Which of the following would it be BEST to include in the report as the reason for the emergency grant?

    A. The police have decided that the fire is of suspicious origin.
    B. Two neighborhood teenagers were seen leaving the fire at the Smiths'.
    C. The apartment of the Smith family has been destroyed by fire.
    D. Mrs. Smith suffers from a heart murmur and cannot climb stairs.

12. Which of the following would it be BEST to accept as verification of the fire?
    A

    A. letter from the friends with whom the Smiths stayed the previous night
    B. photograph of the fire
    C. dated newspaper clipping describing the fire
    D. note from the Smiths' neighbors

13. A report of the Smith family's need for a new apartment must be sent to the center's housing specialist.
    Which of the following recommendations for housing would be MOST appropriate?

    A. Two bedrooms, first floor walk-up
    B. Five rooms, ground floor
    C. Two-room suite, hotel with elevator
    D. Three rooms, building with elevator

11.____

12.____

13.____

14. For which of the following are the Smiths requesting emergency funds? 14.____

    A. Furniture B. Food
    C. A hotel room D. Repairs in their apartment

15. Which of the following statements provides the BEST summary of the action taken by you on the Smith case and is MOST important for inclusion in your report? 15.____

    A. Mr. and Mrs. Smith arrived upset and anxious and were reassured.
    B. It was verified that there was a fire.
    C. Temporary living arrangements were made, and the amount of the emergency grant was determined.
    D. The case was studied and a new apartment was found for the Smiths which met with their approval.

16. It is important that you remember what has happened between you and a client during an interview so that you may deliver appropriate services. 16.____
    However, the one of the following which is the MOST likely reason that taking notes during the interview may not always be a good practice is that

    A. you may lose the notes and have to go back and see the client again
    B. some clients may believe that you are not interested in what they are saying
    C. you are the only one who is likely to read the notes
    D. some clients may believe that you are not smart enough to remember what happened in the interview

17. Before an applicant seeking public assistance can be interviewed, he must fill out a complex application form which consists of eleven pages of questions requesting very detailed information. 17.____
    Of the following, the BEST time for you to review the information on the application form is

    A. before she begins to interview the applicant
    B. after she has asked the applicant a few questions to put him at ease
    C. towards the end of the interview so that she has a chance to think about the information received during the interview
    D. after the interview has been completed

Questions 18-20.

DIRECTIONS: In Questions 18 through 20, choose the lettered word which means MOST NEARLY the same as the underlined word in the sentence.

18. He needed public assistance because he was incapacitated. The word incapacitated means MOST NEARLY 18.____

    A. uneducated B. disabled
    C. uncooperative D. discharged

19. The caseworker explained to the client that signing the document was compulsory. The word compulsory means MOST NEARLY 19.____

    A. temporary B. required
    C. different D. comprehensive

20. The woman's actions did not <u>jeopardize</u> her eligibility for benefits. 20.____
    The word <u>jeopardize</u> means MOST NEARLY
    A. delay   B. reinforce   C. determine   D. endanger

KEY (CORRECT ANSWERS)

1. C
2. C
3. A
4. A
5. C

6. B
7. A
8. B
9. A
10. A

11. C
12. C
13. B
14. B
15. C

16. B
17. A
18. B
19. B
20. D

TEST 2

DIRECTIONS: Each question or incomplete statement is followed by several suggested answers or completions. Select the one that BEST answers the question or completes the statement. *PRINT THE LETTER OF THE CORRECT ANSWER IN THE SPACE AT THE RIGHT.*

Questions 1-4.

DIRECTIONS: Questions 1 through 4 are to be answered on the basis of the information given in the Fact Situation and Sample Form below.

FACT SITUATION

On October 7, 2014, John Smith (Case #ADC-U 1467912) applied and was accepted for public assistance for himself and his family. His family consists of his wife, Helen, and their children: William, age 9; John Jr., age 6; and Mary, age 2. The family has lived in a five-room apartment located at 142 West 137 Street, Manhattan, since July 18, 2008. Mr. Smith signed a 2-year lease for this apartment on July 18, 2014 at a rent of $500 per month. The maximum rental allowance for a family of this size is $420 per month. Utilities are included in this rent-controlled multiple dwelling.

Since the cost of renting this apartment is in excess of the allowable amount, the Supervising Clerk (Income Maintenance) is required to fill out a "Request for Approval of Exception to Policy for Shelter Allowance/Rehousing Expenses."

A sample of a section of this form follows.

SAMPLE FORM

REQUEST FOR APPROVAL OF EXCEPTION TO POLICY FOR SHELTER ALLOWANCE /REHOUSING EXPENSES

Case Name	Case No. or Pending		Acceptance Date	Group No.	
Present Address ZIP	Apt. No. or Location	No. of Rooms	Rent per Mo. $	Occupancy Date	
HOUSEHOLD COMPOSITION (List all persons living in the household) Column I Surname First	Col. 2 Birth-date	Col. 3 Sex	Column 4 Relation to Case Head	Column 5 Marital Status	Column 6 P. A. Status

1. Based on the information given in the Fact Situation, which one of the following should be entered in the space for *Occupancy Date?*

   A. October 7, 2014 B. July 18, 2014
   C. July 18, 2008 D. Unknown

2. What amount should be entered in the space labeled *Rent per Mo.* ?

   A. $500 B. $420 C. $300 D. $80

3. Based on the information given in the Fact Situation, it is IMPOSSIBLE to fill in which one of the following blanks?

   A. *Case Number or pending* B. *Acceptance Date*
   C. *Apt. No. or Location* D. *No. of Rooms*

4. Which of the following should be entered in Column 4 for Helen Smith?

   A. Wife B. Head C. Mother D. Unknown

Questions 5-13.

DIRECTIONS: In Questions 5 through 13, perform the computations indicated and choose the CORRECT answer from the four choices given.

5. Add $4.34, $34.50, $6.00, $101.76, $90.67. From the result, subtract $60.54 and $10.56.

   A. $76.17 B. $156.37 C. $166.17 D. $300.37

6. Add 2,200, 2,600, 252, and 47.96.
   From the result, subtract 202.70, 1,200, 2,150, and 434.43.

   A. 1,112.83 B. 1,213.46 C. 1,341.51 D. 1,348.91

7. Multiply 1850 by .05 and multiply 3300 by .08 and then add both results.

   A. 242.50 B. 264.00 C. 333.25 D. 356.50

8. Multiply 312.77 by .04.
   Round off the result to the nearest hundredth.

   A. 12.52 B. 12.511 C. 12.518 D. 12.51

9. Add 362.05, 91.13, 347.81, and 17.46, and then divide the result by 6.
   The answer rounded off to the nearest hundredth is

   A. 138.409 B. 137.409 C. 136.41 D. 136.40

10. Add 66.25 and 15.06, and then multiply the result by 2 1/6.
    The answer is MOST NEARLY

    A. 176.18 B. 176.17 C. 162.66 D. 162.62

11. Each of the following options contains three decimals. In which case do all three decimals have the same value?

    A. .3; .30; .03 B. .25; .250; .2500
    C. 1.9; 1.90; 1.09 D. .35; .350; .035

12. Add 1/2 the sum of (539.84 and 479.26) to 1/3 the sum of (1461.93 and 927.27). 12.____
    Round off the result to the nearest whole number.

    A. 3408   B. 2899   C. 1816   D. 1306

13. Multiply $5,906.09 by 15%, and then divide the result by 1/3. 13.____

    A. $295.30   B. $885.91   C. $8,859.14   D. $29,530.45

Questions 14-18.

DIRECTIONS: Questions 14 through 18 are to be answered SOLELY on the basis of the information provided in the following passage.

The ideal relationship for the interview is one of mutual confidence. To try to pretend, to put on a front of cordiality and friendship is extremely unwise for the interviewer because he will certainly convey, by subtle means, his real feelings. It is the interviewer's responsibility to take the lead in establishing a relationship of mutual confidence.

As the interviewer, you should help the interviewee to feel at ease and ready to talk. One of the best ways to do this is to be at ease yourself. If you are, it will probably be evident; if you are not, it will almost certainly be apparent to the interviewee.

Begin the interview with topics for discussion which are easy to talk about and non-menacing. This interchange can be like the conversation of people when they are waiting for a bus, at the ball game, or discussing the weather. However, do not prolong this warm-up too long since the interviewee knows as well as you do that these are not the things he came to discuss. Delaying too long in getting down to business may suggest to him that you are reluctant to deal with the topic.

Once you get onto the main topics, do all that you can to get the interviewee to talk freely with as little prodding from you as possible. This will probably require that you give him some idea of the area, and of ways of looking at it. Avoid, however, prejudicing or coloring his remarks by what you say; especially, do not in any way indicate that there are certain things you want to hear, others which you do not want to hear. It is essential that he feel free to express his own ideas unhampered by your ideas, your values and preconceptions.

Do not appear to dominate the interview, nor have even the suggestion of a patronizing attitude. Ask some questions which will enable the interviewee to take pride in his knowledge. Take the attitude that the interviewee sincerely wants the interview to achieve its purpose. This creates a warm, permissive atmosphere that is most important in all interviews.

14. Of the following, the BEST title for the above passage is 14.____

    A. PERMISSIVENESS IN INTERVIEWING
    B. INTERVIEWING TECHNIQUES
    C. THE FACTOR OF PRETENSE IN THE INTERVIEW
    D. THE CORDIAL INTERVIEW

15. Which of the following recommendations on the conduct of an interview is made by the above passage?

    A. Conduct the interview as if it were an interchange between people discussing the weather.
    B. The interview should be conducted in a highly impersonal manner.
    C. Allow enough time for the interview so that the interviewee does not feel rushed.
    D. Start the interview with topics which are not threatening to the interviewee.

16. The above passage indicates that the interviewer should

    A. feel free to express his opinions
    B. patronize the interviewee and display a permissive attitude
    C. permit the interviewee to give the needed information in his own fashion
    D. provide for privacy when conducting the interview

17. The meaning of the word *unhampered,* as it is used in the last sentence of the fourth paragraph of the preceding passage, is MOST NEARLY

    A. unheeded   B. unobstructed
    C. hindered   D. aided

18. It can be INFERRED from the above passage that

    A. interviewers, while generally mature, lack confidence
    B. certain methods in interviewing are more successful than others in obtaining information
    C. there is usually a reluctance on the part of interviewers to deal with unpleasant topics
    D. it is best for the interviewer not to waiver from the use of hard and fast rules when dealing with clients

19. The applicant whom you are interviewing is not talking rationally, and he admits that he is under the influence of alcohol.
    Which of the following is the BEST way of handling this situation?

    A. Call a security guard and have the applicant removed.
    B. Tell the applicant that unless he gets control of himself, he will not receive financial assistance.
    C. Send out for a cup of black coffee for the applicant.
    D. End the interview and plan to schedule another appointment.

20. During an interview, an applicant who has submitted an application for assistance breaks down and cries. Of the following, the BEST way of handling this situation is to

    A. end the interview and schedule a new appointment
    B. be patient and sympathetic, and encourage the applicant to continue the interview
    C. tell the applicant sternly that crying will not help matters
    D. tell the applicant that you will do everything you can to get the application approved

KEY (CORRECT ANSWERS)

1. C
2. A
3. C
4. A
5. C

6. A
7. D
8. D
9. C
10. B

11. B
12. D
13. A
14. B
15. D

16. C
17. B
18. B
19. D
20. B

EXAMINATION SECTION
TEST 1

DIRECTIONS: Each question or incomplete statement is followed by several suggested answers or completions. Select the one that BEST answers the question or completes the statement. *PRINT THE LETTER OF THE CORRECT ANSWER IN THE SPACE AT THE RIGHT.*

1. Assume that an applicant, obviously under a great deal of stress, talks continuously and rambles, making it difficult for you to determine the exact problem and her need. In order to make the interview more successful, it would be BEST for you to
    A. interrupt the applicant and ask her specific questions in order to get the information you need
    B. tell the applicant that her rambling may be a basic cause of her problem
    C. let the applicant continue talking as long as she wishes
    D. ask the applicant to get to the point because other people are waiting for you

1.____

2. A worker must be able to interview clients all day and still be able to listen and maintain interest.
   Of the following, it is MOST important for you to show interest in the client because, if you appear interested,
    A. the client is more likely to appreciate your professional status
    B. the client is more likely to disclose a greater amount of information
    C. the client is less likely to tell lies
    D. you are more likely to gain your supervisor's approval

2.____

3. The application process is overwhelming to applicant Ms. M. She is very anxious and is fearful that she does not have all that she needs to be eligible for assistance. As a result, every time she is asked to produce a verifying document during the interview, she fumbles and drops all the other documents to the floor.
   Of the following, the MOST effective method for you to use to complete the application process is to
    A. ask Ms. M not to be so nervous because you cannot get the work done if she fusses so much
    B. take the documents away from Ms. M and do it your self
    C. suggest that Ms. M get a friend to come and help her with the papers
    D. try to calm Ms. M and tell her that you are willing to help her with the papers to get the information you require

3.____

4. An applicant for public assistance claims that her husband deserted the family and that she needs money immediately for food since her children have not eaten for two days. Under normal procedure, she has to wait several days before she can be given any money for this purpose. In accordance with departmental policy, no exception can be made in this case.
Of the following, the BEST action for you to take is to
   A. tell her that, according to departmental policy, she cannot be given money immediately
   B. purchase some food for her, using your own funds, so that she can feed her children
   C. take up a collection among co-workers
   D. send her to another center

5. Applicants for public assistance often complain about the length of the application form. They also claim that the questions are too personal, since all they want is money. It is true that the form is long, but the answers to all the questions on the form are needed so that the department can make a decision on eligibility.
When applicants complain, which of the following would be the MOST appropriate action for you to take?
   A. Help such applicants understand that each question has a purpose which will help in the determination of eligibility
   B. Tell such applicants that you agree but that you must comply with regulations because it is your job
   C. Tell such applicants that they should stop complaining if they want you to help
   D. Refer such applicants to a supervisor who will explain agency policy

6. Which one of the following statements BEST describes the primary goal of a worker?
   A. Process as many clients in as short a time as possible
   B. Help his clients
   C. Grow into a more understanding person
   D. Assert his authority

7. Restating a question before the person being interviewed gives an answer to the original question is usually NOT good practice *principally* because
   A. the client will think that you don't know your job
   B. it may confuse the client
   C. the interviewer should know exactly what to ask and how to put the question
   D. it reveals the interviewer's insecurity

8. A white worker can BEST improve his ability to work with black clients if he
   A. tries to forget that the clients are black
   B. tells the black clients that he has no prejudices
   C. becomes aware of the problems black clients face
   D. socializes with black workers in the agency

9. A client warns that if he does not get what he wants he will report you to your supervisor and, if necessary, to the mayor's office.
   Of the following, the MOST appropriate response for you to make in this situation is to
   A. encourage the client to do as he threatens because you know that you are right
   B. call your supervisor in so that the client may confront him
   C. explain to the client how the decision will be made on his request and suggest what action he can take if there is an adverse decision
   D. try to understand the client's problem but tell him that he must not explode in the office because you will have to ask him to leave if he does

Questions 10-20.

DIRECTIONS: Refer to the following Semi-Monthly Family Allowance Schedule and Conversion Table when answering Questions 10 through 20.

SEMI-MONTHLY FAMILY ALLOWANCE SCHEDULE
(Based on Number of Persons in Household)

NUMBER OF PERSONS IN HOUSEHOLD						
One	Two	Three	Four	Five	Six	Each Additional Person
$470.00	$750.00	$1000.00	$1290.00	$1590.00	$1840.00	$25.00

CONVERSION TABLE - WEEKLY TO SEMI-MONTHLY AMOUNTS

DOLLARS				CENTS			
Weekly Amount	Semi-Monthly Amount	Weekly Amount	Semi-Monthly Amount	Weekly Amount	Semi-Monthly Amount	Weekly Amount	Semi-Monthly Amount
$10.00	$21.70	$510.00	$1105.00	$0.10	$0.20	$5.10	$11.10
20.00	43.30	520.00	1126.70	0.20	0.40	5.20	11.30
30.00	65.00	530.00	1148.30	0.30	0.70	5.30	11.50
40.00	86.70	540.00	1170.00	0.40	0.90	5.40	11.70
50.00	108.30	550.00	1191.70	0.50	1.10	5.50	11.90
60.00	130.00	560.00	1213.30	0.60	1.30	5.60	12.10
70.00	151.70	570.00	1235.00	0.70	1.50	5.70	12.40
80.00	173.30	580.00	1256.70	0.80	1.70	5.80	12.60
90.00	195.00	590.00	1278.30	0.90	2.00	5.90	12.80
100.00	216.70	600.00	1300.00	1.00	2.20	6.00	13.00
110.00	238.30	610.00	1321.70	1.10	2.40	6.10	13.20
120.00	260.00	620.00	1343.30	1.20	2.60	6.20	13.40
130.00	281.70	630.00	1365.00	1.30	2.80	6.30	13.70
140.00	303.30	640.00	1386.70	1.40	3.00	6.40	13.90
150.00	325.00	650.00	1408.30	1.50	3.30	6.50	14.10
160.00	346.70	660.00	1430.00	1.60	3.50	6.60	14.30
170.00	368.30	670.00	1451.70	1.70	3.70	6.70	14.50
180.00	390.00	680.00	1473.30	1.80	3.90	6.80	14.70
190.00	411.70	690.00	1495.00	1.90	4.10	6.90	15.00
200.00	433.30	700.00	1516.70	2.00	4.30	7.00	15.20
210.00	455.00	710.00	1538.30	2.10	4.60	7.10	15.40
220.00	476.70	720.00	1560.00	2.20	4.80	7.20	15.60
230.00	498.30	730.00	1581.70	2.30	5.00	7.30	15.80
240.00	520.00	740.00	1603.30	2.40	5.20	7.40	16.00
250.00	541.70	750.00	1625.00	2.50	5.40	7.50	16.30
260.00	563.30	760.00	1646.70	2.60	5.60	7.60	16.50
270.00	585.00	770.00	1668.30	2.70	5.90	7.70	16.70
280.00	606.70	780.00	1690.00	2.80	6.10	7.80	16.90
290.00	628.30	790.00	1711.70	2.90	6.30	7.90	17.10
300.00	650.00	800.00	1733.30	3.00	6.50	8.00	17.30
310.00	671.70	810.00	1755.00	3.10	6.70	8.10	17.60
320.00	693.30	820.00	1776.70	3.20	6.90	8.20	17.80
330.00	715.00	830.00	1798.30	3.30	7.20	8.30	18.00
340.00	736.70	840.00	1820.00	3.40	7.40	8.40	18.20
350.00	783.00	850.00	1841.70	3.50	7.60	8.50	18.40
360.00	780.00	860.00	1863.30	3.60	7.80	8.60	18.60
370.00	801.70	870.00	1885.00	3.70	8.00	8.70	18.90
380.00	823.30	880.00	1906.70	3.80	8.20	8.80	19.10
390.00	845.00	890.00	1928.30	3.90	8.50	8.90	18.30
400.00	866.70	900.00	1950.00	4.00	8.70	9.00	19.50
410.00	888.30	910.00	1971.70	4.10	8.90	9.10	19.70
420.00	910.00	920.00	1993.30	4.20	9.10	9.20	19.90
430.00	931.70	930.00	2015.00	4.30	9.30	9.30	20.20
440.00	953.30	940.00	2036.70	4.40	9.50	9.40	20.40
450.00	975.00	950.00	2058.30	4.50	9.80	9.50	20.60
460.00	996.70	960.00	2080.00	4.60	10.00	9.60	20.80
470.00	1018.30	970.00	2101.70	4.70	10.20	9.70	21.00
480.00	1040.00	980.00	2123.30	4.80	10.40	9.80	21.20
490.00	1061.70	990.00	2145.00	4.90	10.60	9.90	21.50
500.00	1083.30	1000.00	2166.70	5.00	10.80		

5 (#1)

NOTE: Questions 10 through 20 are to be answered SOLELY on the basis of the Schedule and Table given above and the information and case situations given below.

Questions 10 through 14 are based on Case Situation #1.
Questions 15 through 20 are based on Case Situation #2.

Public assistance grants are computed on a semi-monthly basis. This means that all figures are first broken down into semi-monthly amounts, and that when a client receives a check twice a month, each semi-monthly check covers his requirements for a period of approximately 2-1/6 weeks. The grants are computed by means of the following procedures.

1. Determine the semi-monthly allowance for the family from the Semi-Monthly Family Allowance Schedule.
2. Determine total semi-monthly income by deducting from the semi-monthly gross earnings (the wages or salary *before* payroll deductions) all semi-monthly expenses for federal, state, and city income taxes, Social Security payments, State Disability Insurance payments, union dues, cost of transportation, and $10.00 per work day for lunch.
3. Add the semi-monthly allowance and the semi-monthly rent (monthly rent must be divided in half).
4. Subtract the semi-monthly income (if there is any income).
5. The formula for computing the semi-monthly grant is:
   Family Allowance + Rent (semi-monthly)
   Total Income (semi-monthly)
   = Amount of Grant (semi-monthly)
6. Refer to the Conversion Table in order to convert weekly amounts into semi-monthly amounts.

CASE SITUATION #1

The Smiths receive public assistance. The family includes John Smith, his wife Barbara, and their four children. They occupy a five-room apartment for which the rent is $1050.00 per month. Mr. Smith is employed as a cleaner and his gross wages are $1000 per week. He is employed 5 days a week and spends $7.00 a day carfare. He buys his lunches. The following weekly deductions are made from his salary:

Social Security	$60.00
Disability Benefits	3.80
Federal Income Tax	43.00
State Income Tax	28.00
City Income Tax	10.00

CASE SITUATION #2

The Jones family receives public assistance. The family includes Steven and Diane Jones and their two children. They occupy a four-room apartment for which the rental is $850.00 a month. Mr. Jones is employed as a handyman, and his gross wages are $900 per week. He is employed 4 days a week and spends $7.00 a day carfare. He buys his lunches. He has the following weekly deductions made from his salary:

Social Security	$40.00
Disability Benefits	2.70
Federal Income Tax	38.90
State Income Tax	20.50
City Income Tax	6.20

10. The weekly amount that Mr. Smith contributes towards Social Security, Disability Benefits, and income taxes is
    A. $313.70   B. $231.40   C. $144.80   D. $106.80

11. The semi-monthly family allowance for the Smith family is
    A. $1290.00   B. $1590.00   C. $1840.00   D. $1845.00

12. What is the total of semi-monthly expenses related to Mr. Smith's employment which will be deducted from semi-monthly gross earnings to compute semi-monthly income?
    A. $497.80   B. $422.00   C. $389.50   D. $229.80

13. Which of the following amounts is the total semi-monthly income for the Smith family?
    A. $2166.70   B. $2000.00   C. $1668.90   D. $1004.40

14. The amount of the grant which the Smith family is entitled to receive is
    A. $2365.00   B. $1840.00   C. $1392.20   D. $696.10

15. The weekly amount that Mr. Jones contributes towards Social Security, Disability Benefits, and income taxes is
    A. $108.30   B. $176.30   C. $234.30   D. $234.70

16. The semi-monthly family allowance for the Jones family is
    A. $750.00   B. $1000.00   C. $1220.00   D. $1290.00

17. The total of semi-monthly expenses related to Mr. Jones' employment which will be deducted from semi-monthly gross earnings is
    A. $172.30   B. $189.30   C. $382.00   D. $407.20

18. Which of the following amounts is the total semi-monthly income for the Jones family? 18._____
      A. $1282.00   B. $1553.20   C. $1568.00   D. $2122.30

19. The grant which the Jones family will receive is 19._____
      A. $147.00   B. $294.00   C. $1290.00   D. $1715.00

20. If Mrs. Jones' monthly rent had been $1050, what would the amount of the grant be? 20._____
      A. $247.00   B. $494.00   C. $772.00   D. $1822.00

KEY (CORRECT ANSWERS)

1. A   11. C
2. B   12. A
3. D   13. C
4. A   14. D
5. A   15. A

6. B   16. D
7. B   17. C
8. C   18. C
9. C   19. A
10. C   20. A

TEST 2

DIRECTIONS: Each question or incomplete statement is followed by several suggested answers or completions. Select the one that BEST answers the question or completes the statement. *PRINT THE LETTER OF THE CORRECT ANSWER IN THE SPACE AT THE RIGHT.*

Questions 1-5.

DIRECTIONS: Each of Questions 1 through 5 consists of information given in outline form and four sentences labeled A, B, C, and D. For each question, choose the one sentence which CORRECTLY expresses the information given in outline form and which also displays PROPER English usage.

1. Client's Name - Joanna Jones
     Number of Children - 3
     Client's Income - None
     Client's Marital Status - Single
     A. Joanna Jones is an unmarried client with three children who have no income.
     B. Joanna Jones, who is single and has no income, a client she has three children.
     C. Joanna Jones, whose three children are clients, is single and has no income.
     D. Joanna Jones, who has three children, is an unmarried client with no income.

1.____

2. Client's Name - Bertha Smith
     Number of Children - 2
     Client's Rent - $1050 per month
     Number of Rooms- 4
     A. Bertha Smith, a client, pays $1050 per month for her four rooms with two children.
     B. Client Bertha Smith has two children and pays $1050 per month for four rooms.
     C. Client Bertha Smith is paying $1050 per month for two children with four rooms.
     D. For four rooms and two children, Client Bertha Smith pays $1050 per month.

2.____

3. Name of Employee - Cynthia Dawes
     Number of Cases Assigned - 9
     Date Cases Were Assigned - 12/16
     Number of Assigned Cases Completed - 8
     A. On December 16, employee Cynthia Dawes was assigned nine cases; she has completed eight of these cases.
     B. Cynthia Dawes, employee on December 16, assigned nine cases, completed eight.
     C. Being employed on December 16, Cynthia Dawes completed eight of nine assigned cases.
     D. Employee Cynthia Dawes, she was assigned nine cases and completed eight, on December 16.

3.____

4. Place of Audit - Broadway Center
     Names of Auditors - Paul Cahn, Raymond Perez
     Date of Audit - 11/20
     Number of Cases Audited - 41
     A. On November 20, at the Broadway Center 41 cases was audited by auditors Paul Cahn and Raymond Perez.
     B. Auditors Raymond Perez and Paul Cahn has audited 41 cases at the Broadway

4.____

Center, on November 20.
- C. At the Broadway Center, on November 20, auditors Paul Cahn and Raymond Perez audited 41 cases.
- D. Auditors Paul Cahn and Raymond Perez at the Broadway Center, on November 20, is auditing 41 cases.

5. Name of Client - Barbra Levine 5.____
   Client's Monthly Income - $2100
   Client's Monthly Expenses - $4520
   - A. Barbra Levine is a client, her monthly income is $2100 and her monthly expenses is $4520.
   - B. Barbra Levine's monthly income is $2100 and she is a client, with whose monthly expenses are $4520.
   - C. Barbra Levine is a client whose monthly income is $2100 and whose monthly expenses are $4520.
   - D. Barbra Levine, a client, is with a monthly income which is $2100 and monthly expenses which are $4520.

Questions 6-10.

DIRECTIONS: Questions 6 through 10 are to be answered SOLELY on the basis of the information contained in the following passage.

Any person who is living in New York City and is otherwise eligible may be granted public assistance whether or not he has New York State residence. However, since New York City does not contribute to the cost of assistance granted to persons who are without State residence, the cases of all recipients must be formally identified as to whether or not each member of the household has State residence.

To acquire State residence a person must have resided in New York State continuously for one year. Such residence is not lost unless the person is out of the State continuously for a period of one year or longer. Continuous residence does not include any period during which the individual is a patient in a hospital, an inmate of a public institution or of an incorporated private institution, a resident on a military reservation or a minor residing in a boarding home while under the care of an authorized agency. Receipt of public assistance does not prevent a person from acquiring State residence. State residence, once acquired, is not lost because of absence from the State while a person is serving in the U.S. Armed Forces or the Merchant Marine; nor does a member of the family of such a person lose State residence while living with or near that person in these circumstances.

Each person, regardless of age, acquires or loses State residence as an individual. There is no derivative State residence except for an infant at the time of birth. He is deemed to have State residence if he is in the custody of both parents and either one of them has State residence, or if the parent having custody of him has State residence.

6. According to the above passage, an infant is deemed to have New York State residence at the time of his birth *if*
   A. he is born in New York State but neither of his parents is a resident
   B. he is in the custody of only one parent, who is not a resident, but his other parent is a resident
   C. his brother and sister are residents
   D. he is in the custody of both his parents but only one of them is a resident

7. The Jones family consists of five members. Jack and Mary Jones have lived in New York State continuously for the past eighteen months after having lived in Ohio since they were born. Of their three children, one was born ten months ago and has been in the custody of his parents since birth. Their second child lived in Ohio until six months ago and then moved in with his parents. Their third child had never lived in New York until he moved with his parents to New York eighteen months ago. However, he entered the armed forces one month later and has not lived in New York since that time.
   Based on the above passage, how many members of the Jones family are New York State residents?
   A. 2   B. 3   C. 4   D. 5

8. Assuming that each of the following individuals has lived continuously in New York State for the past year, and has never previously lived in the State, which one of them is a New York State resident?
   A. Jack Salinas, who has been an inmate in a State correctional facility for six months of the year
   B. Fran Johnson, who has lived on an Army base for the entire year
   C. Arlene Snyder, who married a non-resident during the past year
   D. Gary Phillips, who was a patient in a Veterans Administration hospital for the entire year

9. The above passage implies that the reason for determining whether or not a recipient of public assistance is a State resident is that
   A. the cost of assistance for non-residents is not a New York City responsibility
   B. non-residents living in New York City are not eligible for public assistance
   C. recipients of public assistance are barred from acquiring State residence
   D. New York City is responsible for the full cost of assistance to recipients who are residents

10. Assume that the Rollins household in New York City consists of six members at the present time - Anne Rollins, her three children, her aunt and her uncle. Anne Rollins and one of her children moved to New York City seven months ago. Neither of them had previously lived in New York State. Her other two children have lived in New York City continuously for the past two years, as has her aunt. Anne Rollins' uncle had lived in New York City continuously for many years until two years ago. He then entered the armed forces and has returned to New York City within the past month.
    Based on the above passage, how many members of the Rollins' household are New York State residents?
    A. 2   B. 3   C. 4   D. 6

11. You are interviewing a client to determine whether financial assistance should be continued and   11.____
you find that what he is telling you does not agree exactly with your records.
Of the following, the BEST way to handle this situation is to
   A. recommend that his public assistance payments be stopped, since you have caught him lying to you
   B. tell the client about the points of disagreement and ask him if he can clear them up
   C. give the client the benefit of the doubt and recommend continuation of his payments
   D. show the client the records and warn him that he must either tell the truth or lose his benefits

12. An applicant for public assistance gets angry at some of the questions you must ask her.   12.____
Of the following, the BEST way to handle this situation is to
   A. assume that she is trying to hide something, and end the interview
   B. skip the questions that bother her and come back to them at the end of the interview
   C. tell her that she must either answer the question or leave
   D. explain to her that you are required to get answers to all the questions in order to be able to help her

13. At the end of an interview to determine whether financial assistance should be continued, the client   13.____
offers to take you to lunch.
Of the following, the BEST response to such an invitation is to
   A. tell the client that you do not take bribes and report the matter to your supervisor
   B. accept the invitation if you have the time, but do not let it influence your recommendation as to his eligibility for continuing public assistance
   C. politely refuse the invitation, and do not let it influence your recommendation as to his continuing eligibility for public assistance
   D. point out to the client that his budget does not include money for entertainment

Questions 14-18.

DIRECTIONS: Questions 14 through 18 are to be answered SOLELY on the basis of the information, the assumptions, and the table given below.

Each question describes an applicant family. You are to determine into which of the four categories (A, B, C, or D) each of the applicant families should be placed. In order to do this, you must match the description of the applicant family with the factors determining eligibility for each of the four categories. Each applicant family must meet ALL of the criteria for the category.

ASSUMPTIONS FOR ALL QUESTIONS
The information in the following tables does NOT necessarily reflect actual practice in the Department of Social Services.
   1. The date of application is January 25.
   Each applicant family that cannot be placed in categories A, B, or C must be placed in category D.
   2. A *dependent child* is a child who is less than 18 years of age, or less than 21 years of age if attending school full time, who depends upon its parents for support.
   3. A mother in a family with one or more dependent children is not expected to work and her work status is not to be considered in establishing the category of the family.

CATEGORY OF APPLICANT FAMILY	FACTORS DETERMINING ELIGIBILITY

A	1. There is at least one dependent child in the home.
	2. Children are deprived of parental support because father is:
	   (a) Deceased
	   (b) Absent from the home
	   (c) Incapacitated due to medically verified illness
	   (d) Over age 65
	   (e) Not fully employed because of verified ill health
	3. Parents or guardians reside in the same home as the children.
	4. Applicant family must have resided in the State for a period of one year or more.

B	1. There is at least one dependent child in the home. 2. Both parents are in the home and are not incapacitated. 3. Both parents are the children's natural parents. 4. Father unemployed or works less than 70 hours per month. 5. Father has recent work history. 6. Father not currently receiving Unemployment Insurance Benefits. 7. Father available and willing to work. 8. Applicant family must have resided in the State for a period of one year or more.
C	1. There is a war veteran in the home. 2. Applicant families do not meet the criteria for Categories A or B.
D	Applicant families do not meet the criteria for Categories A, B, or C

14. Woman, aged 52, with child 6 years old who she states was left in her home at the age of 2. Woman states child is her niece, and that she has no knowledge of whereabouts of parents or any other relatives. Both woman and child have resided in the State since June 15.   14. ___

15. Married couple with 2 dependent children at home. Family has resided in the State for the last 5 years. Wife cannot work. Husband, veteran of Gulf War, can work only 15 hours a week due to kidney ailment (verified).   15. ___

16. Married couple, both aged 35, with 3 dependent children at home, 1 of whom is 17 years of age. Wife available for work and presently working 2 days a week, 7 hours each day. Husband, who was laid off two weeks ago, is not eligible for Unemployment Insurance Benefits. Family has resided in the State since January 1, 2002.

16. _____

17. Married couple with 1 dependent child at home. They have resided in the State since January 25, 2001. Wife must remain home to take care of child. Husband veteran of Gulf War. Husband is available for work on a limited basis because of heart condition which has been verified. A second child, a married 17-year-old son, lives in California.

17. _____

18. Married couple with 2 children, ages 6 and 12, at home. Family has resided in the State since June 2, 1998. Wife not available for work. Husband, who served in the Iraqi War, was laid off 3 weeks ago and is receiving Unemployment Insurance Benefits of $500.00 weekly.

18. _____

19. Of the following, the MOST important reason for referring a public assistance client for employment or training is to
    A. give him self-confidence
    B. make him self-supporting
    C. have him learn a new trade
    D. take him off the streets

19. _____

20. Sometimes clients become silent during interviews.
    Of the following, the MOST probable reason for such silence is that the client is
    A. getting ready to tell a lie
    B. of low intelligence and does not know the answers to your questions
    C. thinking things over or has nothing more to say on the subject
    D. wishing he were not on welfare

20. _____

KEY (CORRECT ANSWERS)

1. D	6. D	11. B	16. B
2. B	7. B	12. D	17. A
3. A	8. C	13. C	18. C
4. C	9. A	14. D	19. B
5. C	10. C	15. A	20. C

EXAMINATION SECTION
TEST 1

DIRECTIONS: Each question or incomplete statement is followed by several suggested answers or completions. Select the one that BEST answers the question or completes the statement. *PRINT THE LETTER OF THE CORRECT ANSWER IN THE SPACE AT THE RIGHT.*

Questions 1-10.

DIRECTIONS: For each of the sentences given below, numbered 1 through 10, select from the following choices the MOST correct choice and print your choice in the space at the right. Select as your answer:
- A – if the statement contains an unnecessary word of expression
- B – if the statement contains a slang term or expression ordinarily not acceptable in government report writing
- C – if the statement contains an old-fashioned word or expression, where a concrete, plain term would be more useful
- D – if the statement contains no major faults

1. Every one of us should try harder.
2. Yours of the first instant has been received.
3. We will have to do a real snow job on him.
4. I shall contact him next Thursday.
5. None of us were invited to the meeting with the community.
6. We got this here job to do.
7. She could not help but see the mistake in the checkbook.
8. Don't bug the Director about the report.
9. I beg to inform you that your letter has been received.
10. This project is all screwed up.

Questions 11-15.

DIRECTIONS: Read the following Inter-office Memo. Then answer Questions 11 through 15 based ONLY on the memo.

INTER-OFFICE MEMORANDUM

To: Alma Robinson, Human Resources Aide
From: Frank Shields, Social Worker

I would like to have you help Mr. Edward Tunney who is trying to raise his two children by himself. He needs to learn to improve the physical care of his children and especially of his daughter Helen, age 9. She is avoided and ridiculed at school because her hair is uncombed, her teeth not properly cleaned, her clothing torn, wrinkled and dirty, as well as shabby and poorly fitted. The teachers and school officials have contacted the Department and the social worker for two years about Helen. She is not able to make friends because of these problems. I have talked to Mr. Tunney about improvements for the child's clothing, hair, and hygiene. He tends to deny these things are problems, but is cooperative, and a second person showing him the importance of better physical care for Helen would be helpful.

Perhaps you could teach Helen how to fix her own hair. She has all the materials. I would also like you to form your own opinion of the sanitary conditions in the home and how they could be improved.

Mr. Tunney is expecting your visit and is willing to talk with you about ways he can help with these problems.

11. In the above memorandum, the Human Resources Aide is being asked to help Mr. Tunney to

    A. improve the learning habits of his children
    B. enable his children to make friends at school
    C. take responsibility for the upbringing of his children
    D. give attention to the grooming and cleanliness of his children

12. This case was brought to the attention of the social worker by

    A. government officials
    B. teachers and school officials
    C. the Department
    D. Mr. Tunney

13. In general, Mr. Tunney's attitude with regard to his children could BEST be described as

    A. interested in correcting the obvious problems, but unable to do so alone
    B. unwilling to follow the advice of those who are trying to help
    C. concerned, but unaware of the seriousness of these problems
    D. interested in helping them, but afraid of taking the advice of the social worker

14. Which of the following actions has NOT been suggested as a possible step for the Human Resources Aide to take?

    A. Help Helen to learn to care for herself by teaching her grooming skills
    B. Determine ways of improvement through information gathered on a home visit
    C. Discuss her own views on Helen's problems with school officials
    D. Ask Mr. Tunney in what ways he believes the physical care may be improved

15. According to the memo, the Human Resources Aide is ESPECIALLY being asked to observe and form her own opinions about   15._____

    A. the relationship between Mr. Tunney and the school officials
    B. Helen's attitude toward her classmates and teacher
    C. the sanitary conditions in the home
    D. the reasons Mr. Tunney is not cooperative with the agency

16. In one day, an aide receives 18 inquiries by phone and 27 inquiries in person. What percentage of the inquiries received that day were by phone?   16._____

    A. 33%   B. 40%   C. 45%   D. 60%

17. If the weekly pay checks for 5 part-time employees are: $129.32, $162.74, $143.67, $135.75, and $156.56, then the combined weekly income for the 5 employees is   17._____

    A. $727.84   B. $728.04   C. $730.84   D. $737.04

18. Suppose that there are 17 aides working in an office where many community complaints are received by telephone. In one ten-day period, 4250 calls were received. If the same number of calls were received each day, and the aides divided the work load equally, about how many calls did each aide respond to daily?   18._____

    A. 25   B. 35   C. 75   D. 250

19. Suppose that an assignment was divided among 5 aides. If the first aide spent 67 hours on the assignment, the second aide spent 95 hours, the third aide spent 52 hours, the fourth aide spent 78 hours, and the fifth aide spent 103 hours, what was the AVERAGE amount of time spent by each aide on the assignment?   19._____
    _____ hours.

    A. 71   B. 75   C. 79   D. 83

20. If there are 240 employees in a center and 1/3 are absent on the day of a bad snowstorm, how many employees were at work in the center on that day?   20._____

    A. 80   B. 120   C. 160   D. 200

KEY (CORRECT ANSWERS)

1. D
2. C
3. B
4. D
5. D

6. B
7. D
8. B
9. C
10. B

11. D
12. B
13. C
14. C
15. C

16. B
17. B
18. A
19. C
20. C

TEST 2

DIRECTIONS: Each question or incomplete statement is followed by several suggested answers or completions. Select the one that BEST answers the question or completes the statement. *PRINT THE LETTER OF THE CORRECT ANSWER IN THE SPACE AT THE RIGHT.*

1. Suppose that an aide takes 25 minutes to prepare a letter to a client.
   If the aide is assigned to prepare 9 letters on a certain day, how much time should she set aside for this task? _____ hours.

   A. 3 3/4   B. 4 1/4   C. 4 3/4   D. 5 1/4

   1._____

2. Suppose that a certain center uses both Form A and Form B in the course of its daily work, and that Form A is used 4 times as often as Form B.
   If the total number of both forms used in one week is 750, how many times was Form A used?

   A. 100   B. 200   C. 400   D. 600

   2._____

3. Suppose a center has a budget of $1092.70 from which 8 desks costing $78.05 apiece must be bought?
   How many ADDITIONAL desks can be ordered from this budget after the 8 desks have been purchased?

   A. 4   B. 6   C. 9   D. 14

   3._____

4. When researching a particular case, a team of 16 aides was asked to check through 234 folders to obtain the necessary information.
   If half the aides worked twice as fast as the other half, and the slow group checked through 12 folders each hour, about how long would it take to complete the assignment? _____ hours.

   A. $4\frac{1}{4}$ B. 5   C. 6   D. $6\frac{1}{2}$

   4._____

5. The difference in the cost of two printers is $28.32. If the less expensive printer costs $153.61, what is the cost of the other printer?

   A. $171.93   B. $172.03   C. $181.93   D. $182.03

   5._____

Questions 6-8.

DIRECTIONS: Questions 6 through 8 are to be answered on the basis of the following information contained on a sample page of a payroll book.

Emp. No.	Name of Employee	Hours Worked M	T	W	Th	F	Total Hours Worked	Pay PerHour	Total Wages
1	James Smith	8	8	8	8	8			$480.00
2	Gloria Jones	8	7 3/4	7		7 1/2		$16.00	$560.00
3	Robert Adams	6	6	7 1/2	7 1/2	8 3/4		$18.28	

6. The pay per hour of Employee No. 1 is   6._____

   A. $12.00   B. $13.72   C. $15.00   D. $19.20

7. The number of hours that Employee No. 2 worked on Friday is   7._____

   A. 4   B. 5 1/2   C. 4.63   D. 4 3/4

8. The total wages for Employee No. 3 is   8._____

   A. $636.92   B. $648.94   C. $661.04   D. $672.96

9. As a rule, the FIRST step in writing a check should be to   9._____

   A. number the check
   B. write in the payee's name
   C. tear out the check stub
   D. write the purpose of the check in the space provided at the bottom

10. If an error is made when writing a check, the MOST widely accepted procedure is to   10._____

    A. draw a line through the error and initial it
    B. destroy both the check and check stub by tearing into small pieces
    C. erase the error if it does not occur in the amount of the check
    D. write *Void* across both the check and check stub and save them

11. The check that is MOST easily cashed is one that is   11._____

    A. not signed
    B. made payable to *Cash*
    C. post-dated
    D. endorsed in part

12.   12._____

No. 103	$ 142.77
May 14	
To Alan Jacobs	
For Wages (5/6-5/10)	
Bal. Bro't For'd	2340.63
Amt. Deposited	205.24
Total	
Amt. This Check	142.77
Bal. Car'd For'd	

The balance to be carried forward on the check stub above is
    A. $2,278.16   B. $1,992.62   C. $2,688.64   D. $2,403.10

13. The procedure for reconciling a bank statement consists of _____ the bank balance and _____ the checkbook balance.   13._____

    A. *adding* outstanding checks to; *subtracting* the service and check charges from
    B. *subtracting* the service charge from; *subtracting* outstanding checks from
    C. *subtracting* the service charge from; *adding* outstanding checks to
    D. *subtracting* outstanding checks from; *subtracting* the service and check charges from

14. An employee makes $15.70 an hour and receives time-and-a-half in overtime pay for every hour more than 40 in a given week. If the employee works 47 hours, the employee's total wages for that week would be

    A. $792.85 B. $837.90 C. $875.25 D. $1,106.85

15. A high-speed copier can make 25,000 copies before periodic service is required. Before this service is necessary, _____ copies of a 137-page document can be printed.

    A. 211 B. 204 C. 190 D. 178

16. An aide is typing a letter to the James Weldon Johnson Head Start Center. To be sure that a Mr. Joseph Maxwell reads it, an attention line is typed below the inside address. The salutation should, therefore, read:

    A. To Whom It May Concern: B. Dear Mr. Maxwell:
    C. Gentlemen: D. Dear Joseph:

17. When describing the advantages of the numeric filing system, it is NOT true that it

    A. is the most accurate of all methods
    B. allows for unlimited expansion according to the needs of the agency
    C. is a system useful for filing letters directly according to name or subject
    D. allows for cross-referencing

18. In writing a letter for your Center, the PURPOSE of the letter should usually be stated in

    A. the first paragraph. This assists the reader in making more sense of the letter.
    B. the second paragraph. The first paragraph should be used to confirm receipt of the letter being answered
    C. the last paragraph. The first paragraphs should be used to build up to the purpose of the letter.
    D. any paragraph. Each letter has a different purpose and the letter should conform to that purpose.

19. If you open a personal letter addressed to another aide by mistake, the one of the following actions which it would generally be BEST for you to take is to

    A. reseal the envelope or place the contents in another envelope and pass it on to the employee
    B. place the letter inside the envelope, indicate under your initials that it was opened in error and give it to the employee
    C. personally give the employee the letter without any explanation
    D. ignore your error, attach the envelope to the letter, and give it out in the usual manner

20. Of the following, the MAIN purpose of the head start program is to

    A. provide programs for pre-school development of children
    B. provide children between the ages of 6 and 12 with after-school activity
    C. establish a system for providing care for teenage youngsters with working parents
    D. supervise centers providing 24-hour child care

KEY (CORRECT ANSWERS)

1.	A	11.	B
2.	D	12.	D
3.	B	13.	D
4.	D	14.	A
5.	C	15.	D
6.	A	16.	C
7.	D	17.	C
8.	B	18.	A
9.	A	19.	B
10.	D	20.	A

EXAMINATION SECTION
TEST 1

DIRECTIONS: Each question or incomplete statement is followed by several suggested answers or completions. Select the one that BEST answers the question or completes the statement. *PRINT THE LETTER OF THE CORRECT ANSWER IN THE SPACE AT THE RIGHT.*

Questions 1-5.

DIRECTIONS: Questions 1 through 5 consist of a sentence with an underlined word. For each question, select the choice that is CLOSEST in meaning to the underlined word.

EXAMPLE
This division reviews the fiscal reports of the agency.
In this sentence, the word *fiscal* means MOST NEARLY
    A. financial   B. critical   C. basic   D. personnel
The correct answer is A. "financial" because "financial" is closest to *fiscal*. Therefore, the answer is A.

1. Every good office worker needs basic skills.
   The word *basic* in this sentence means
       A. fundamental   B. advanced   C. unusual   D. outstanding

2. He turned out to be a good instructor.
   The word *instructor* in this sentence means
       A. student   B. worker   C. typist   D. teacher

3. The quantity of work in the office was under study.
   In this sentence, the word *quantity* means
       A. amount   B. flow   C. supervision   D. type

4. The morning was spent examining the time records.
   In this sentence, the word *examining* means
       A. distributing   B. collecting   C. checking   D. filing

5. The candidate filled in the proper spaces on the form.
   In this sentence, the word *proper* means
       A. blank   B. appropriate   C. many   D. remaining

Questions 6-8.

DIRECTIONS: Questions 6 through 8 are to be answered SOLELY on the basis of the information contained in the following paragraph.

   The increase in the number of public documents in the last two centuries closely matches the increase in population in the United States. The great number of public documents has become a serious threat to their usefulness. It is necessary to have programs which will reduce the number of public documents that are kept and which will, at the same time, assure keeping those that have value. Such programs need a great deal of thought to have any success.

6. According to the above paragraph, public documents may be less useful if 6.____
   A. the files are open to the public
   B. the record room is too small
   C. the copying machine is operated only during normal working hours
   D. too many records are being kept

7. According to the above paragraph, the growth of the population in the United 7.____
   States has matched the growth in the quantity of public documents for a period
   of MOST NEARLY _____ years.
   A. 50   B. 100   C. 200   D. 300

8. According to the above paragraph, the increased number of public documents 8.____
   has made it necessary to
   A. find out which public documents are worth keeping
   B. reduce the great number of public documents by decreasing government services
   C. eliminate the copying of all original public documents
   D. avoid all new copying devices

Questions 9-10.

DIRECTIONS: Questions 9 and 10 are to be answered SOLELY on the basis of the information contained in the following paragraph.

   The work goals of an agency can best be reached if the employees understand and agree with these goals. One way to gain such understanding and agreement is for management to encourage and seriously consider suggestions from employees in the setting of agency goals.

9. On the basis of the above paragraph, the BEST way to achieve the work goals 9.____
   of an agency is to
   A. make certain that employees work as hard as possible
   B. study the organizational structure of the agency
   C. encourage employees to think seriously about the agency's problems
   D. stimulate employee understanding of the work goals

10. On the basis of the above paragraph, understanding and agreement with agency   10.____
    goals can be gained by
    A. allowing the employees to set agency goals
    B. reaching agency goals quickly
    C. legislative review of agency operations
    D. employee participation in setting agency goals

Questions 11-15.

DIRECTIONS: Each of Questions 11 through 15 consists of a group of four words. One word in each group is incorrectly spelled. For each question, print the letter of the correct answer in the space at the right that is the same as the letter next to the word which is INCORRECTLY spelled.

EXAMPLE

A. housing   B. certain   C. budgit   D. money

The word "budgit" is incorrectly spelled, because the correct spelling should be "budget." Therefore, the correct answer is C.

11.	A. sentince	B. bulletin	C. notice	D. definition	11.____
12.	A. appointment	B. exactly	C. typest	D. light	12.____
13.	A. penalty	B. suparvise	C. consider	D. division	13.____
14.	A. schedule	B. accurate	C. corect	D. simple	14.____
15.	A. suggestion	B. installed	C. proper	D. agincy	15.____

Questions 16-20.

DIRECTIONS: Each Question 16 through 20 consists of a sentence which may be
   A. incorrect because of bad word usage, or
   B. incorrect because of bad punctuation, or
   C. incorrect because of bad spelling, or
   D. correct
Read each sentence carefully. Then print in the space at the right A, B, C, or D, according to the answer you choose from the four choices listed above. There is only one type of error in each incorrect sentence. If there is no error, the sentence is correct.

EXAMPLE

George Washington was the father of his contry.
This sentence is incorrect because of bad spelling ("contry" instead of "country").
Therefore, the answer is C.

4 (#1)

16. The assignment was completed in record time but the payroll for it has not yet been preparid.   16._____

17. The operator, on the other hand, is willing to learn me how to use the mimeograph.   17._____

18. She is the prettiest of the three sisters.   18._____

19. She doesn't know; if the mail has arrived.   19._____

20. The doorknob of the office door is broke.   20._____

21. A clerk can process a form in 15 minutes.
How many forms can that clerk process in six hours?
A. 10   B. 21   C. 24   D. 90   21._____

22. An office staff consists of 120 people. Sixty of them have been assigned to a special project. Of the remaining staff, 20 answer the mail, 10 handle phone calls, and the rest operate the office machines.
The number of people operating the office machines is
A. 20   B. 30   C. 40   D. 45   22._____

23. An office worker received 65 applications but on the first day had to return 26 of them for being incomplete and on the second day 25 had to be returned for being incomplete.
How many applications did NOT have to be returned?
A. 10   B. 12   C. 14   D. 16   23._____

24. An office worker answered 63 phone calls in one day and 91 phone calls the next day.
For these 2 days, what was the average number of phone calls he answered per day?
A. 77   B. 28   C. 82   D. 93   24._____

25. An office worker processed 12 vouchers of $8.50 each, 3 vouchers of $3.68 each, and 2 vouchers of $1.29 each.
The TOTAL dollar amount of these vouchers is
A. $116.04   B. $117.52   C. $118.62   D. $119.04   25._____

KEY (CORRECT ANSWERS)

1. A
2. D
3. A
4. C
5. B

6. D
7. C
8. A
9. D
10. D

11. A
12. C
13. B
14. C
15. D

16. C
17. A
18. D
19. B
20. A

21. C
22. B
23. C
24. A
25. C

TEST 2

DIRECTIONS: Each question or incomplete statement is followed by several suggested answers or completions. Select the one that BEST answers the question or completes the statement. *PRINT THE LETTER OF THE CORRECT ANSWER IN THE SPACE AT THE RIGHT.*

Questions 1-5.

DIRECTIONS: Each Question from 1 through 5 lists four names. The names may not be exactly the same. Compare the names in each question and mark your answer
- A if all the names are different
- B if only two names are exactly the same
- C if only three names are exactly the same
- D if all four names are exactly the same

EXAMPLE
Jensen, Alfred E.
Jensen, Alfred E.
Jensan, Alfred E.
Jensen, Fred E.

Since the name Jensen, Alfred E. appears twice and is exactly the same in both places, the correct answer is B.

1. A. Riviera, Pedro S.   B. Rivers, Pedro S.   1.____
   C. Riviera, Pedro N.   D. Riviera, Juan S.

2. A. Guider, Albert   B. Guidar, Albert   2.____
   C. Giuder, Alfred   D. Guider, Albert

3. A. Blum, Rona   B. Blum, Rona   3.____
   C. Blum, Rona   D. Blum, Rona

4. A. Raugh, John   B. Raugh, James   4.____
   C. Raughe, John   D. Raugh, John

5. A. Katz, Stanley   B. Katz, Stanley   5.____
   C. Katze, Stanley   D. Katz, Stanley

Questions 6-10.

DIRECTIONS: Each Question 6 through 10 consists of numbers or letters in Columns I and II. For each question, compare each line of Column I with its corresponding line in Column II and decide how many lines in Column I are EXACTLY the same as their corresponding lines in Column II. In your answer space, mark your answer
- A if only ONE line in Column I is exactly the same as its corresponding line in Column II
- B if only TWO lines in Column I are exactly the same as their corresponding lines in Column II

2 (#2)

    C if only THREE lines in Column I are exactly the same as their corresponding lines in Column II
    D if all FOUR lines in Column I are exactly the same as their corresponding lines in Column II

EXAMPLE

Column I	Column II
1776	1776
1865	1865
1945	1945
1976	1978

Only three lines in Column I are exactly the same as their corresponding lines in Column II. Therefore, the correct answer is C.

	Column I	Column II	
6.	5653 8727 ZPSS 4952	5653 8728 ZPSS 9453	6.____
7.	PNJP NJPJ JNPN PNJP	PNPJ NJPJ JNPN PNPJ	7.____
8.	effe uWvw KpGj vmnv	eFfe uWvw KpGg vmnv	8.____
9.	5232 PfrC zssz rwwr	5232 PfrN zzss rwww	9.____
10.	czws cecc thrm lwtz	czws cece thrm lwtz	10.____

Questions 11-15.

DIRECTIONS: Questions 11 through 15 have lines of letters and numbers. Each letter should be matched with its number in accordance with the following table.

Letter	F	R	C	A	W	L	E	N	B	T
Matching Number	0	1	2	3	4	5	6	7	8	9

From the table you can determine that the letter F has the matching number 0 below it, the letter R has the matching number 1 below, etc.

For each question, compare each line of letters and numbers carefully to see if each letter has its correct matching number. If all the letters and numbers are matched correctly in

none of the lines of the question, mark your answer A
only *one* of the lines of the question, mark your answer B
only *two* of the lines of the question, mark your answer C
all three lines of the question, mark your answer D

EXAMPLE

WBCR	4826
TLBF	9580
ATNE	3986

There is a mistake in the first line because the letter R should have its matching number 1 instead of the number 6.

The second line is correct because each letter shown has the correct matching number.

There is a mistake in the third line because the letter N should have the matching number 7 instead of the number 8.

Since all the letters and numbers are correct matched in only one of the lines in the sample, the correct answer is B.

11.
    EBCT   6829
    ATWR   3961
    NLBW   7584   11.____

12.
    RNCT   1729
    LNCR   5728
    WAEB   5368   12.____

13.
    NTWB   7948
    RABL   1385
    TAEF   9360   13.____

14.
    LWRB   5417
    RLWN   1647
    CBWA   2843   14.____

15.
    ABTC   3792
    WCER   5261
    AWCN   3417   15.____

16. Your job often brings you into contact with the public.
Of the following, it would be MOST desirable to explain the reasons for official actions to people coming into your office for assistance because such explanations
    A. help build greater understanding between the public and your agency
    B. help build greater self-confidence in city employees
    C. convince the public that nothing they do can upset a city employee
    D. show the public that city employees are intelligent

16.____

17. Assume that you strongly dislike one of your co-workers.
    You should FIRST
    A. discuss your feeling with the co-worker
    B. demand a transfer to another office
    C. suggest to your supervisor that the co-worker should be observed carefully
    D. try to figure out the reason for this dislike before you say or do anything

18. An office worker who has problems accepting authority is MOST likely to find it difficult to
    A. obey rules
    B. understand people
    C. assist other employees
    D. follow complex instructions

19. The employees in your office have taken a dislike to one person and frequently annoy her.
    Your supervisor should
    A. transfer this person to another unit at the first opportunity
    B. try to find out the reason for the staff's attitude before doing anything about it
    C. threaten to transfer the first person observed bothering this person
    D. ignore the situation

20. Assume that your supervisor has asked a worker in your office to get a copy of a report out of the files. You notice the worker as accidentally pulled out the wrong report.
    Of the following, the BEST way for you to handle this situation is to tell
    A. the worker about all the difficulties that will result from this error
    B. the worker about her mistake in a nice way
    C. the worker to ignore this error
    D. your supervisor that this worker needs more training in how to use the files

21. Filing systems differ in their efficiency.
    Which of the following is the BEST way to evaluate the efficiency of a filing system? A
    A. number of times used per day
    B. amount of material that is received each day for filing
    C. amount of time it takes to locate material
    D. type of locking system used

22. In planning ahead so that a sufficient amount of general office supplies is always available, it would be LEAST important to find out the
    A. current office supply needs of the staff
    B. amount of office supplies used last year
    C. days and times that office supplies can be ordered
    D. agency goals and objectives

23. The MAIN reason for establishing routine office work procedures is that once a routine is established
    A. work need not be checked for accuracy
    B. all steps in the routine will take an equal amount of time to perform
    C. each time the job is repeated, it will take less time to perform
    D. each step in the routine will not have to be planned all over again each time

23.____

24. When an office machine centrally located in an agency must be shut down for repairs, the bureaus and divisions using this machine should be informed of the
    A. expected length of time before the machine will be in operation again
    B. estimated cost of repairs
    C. efforts being made to avoid future repairs
    D. type of new equipment which the agency may buy in the future to replace the machine being repaired

24.____

25. If the day's work is properly scheduled, the MOST important result would be that the
    A. supervisor will not have to do much supervision
    B. employee will know what to do next
    C. employee will show greater initiative
    D. job will become routine

25.____

KEY (CORRECT ANSWERS)

1.	A	11.	C
2.	B	12.	B
3.	D	13.	D
4.	B	14.	B
5.	C	15.	A
6.	B	16.	A
7.	B	17.	D
8.	B	18.	A
9.	A	19.	B
10.	C	20.	B

21. C
22. D
23. D
24. A
25. B

INTERVIEWING

EXAMINATION SECTION

TEST 1

DIRECTIONS: Each question or incomplete statement is followed by several suggested answers or completions. Select the one that BEST answers the question or completes the statement. *PRINT THE LETTER OF THE CORRECT ANSWER IN THE SPACE AT THE RIGHT.*

1. Of the following, the MAIN advantage to the supervisor of using the indirect (or nondirective) interview, in which he asks only guiding questions and encourages the employee to do most of the talking, is that he can
   A. obtain a mass of information about the employee in a very short period of time
   B. easily get at facts which the employee wishes to conceal
   C. get answers which are not slanted or biased in order to win his favor
   D. effectively deal with an employee's serious emotional problems

   1.____

2. An interviewer under your supervision routinely closes his interview with a reassuring remark such as, "I'm sure you soon will be well," or "Everything will soon be all right."
   This practice is USUALLY considered
   A. *advisable*, chiefly because the interviewer may make the patient feel better
   B. *inadvisable*, chiefly because it may cause a patient who is seriously ill to doubt the worker's understanding of the situation
   C. *advisable*, chiefly because the patient becomes more receptive if further interviews are needed
   D. *inadvisable*, chiefly because the interviewer should usually not show that he is emotionally involved

   2.____

3. An interviewer has just ushered out a client he has interviewed. As the interviewer is preparing to leave, the client mentions a fact that seems to contradict the information he has given.
   Of the following, it would be BEST for the interviewer at this time to
   A. make no response but write the fact down in his report and plan to come back another day
   B. point out to the client that he has contradicted himself and ask for an explanation
   C. ask the client to elaborate on the comment and attempt to find out further information about the fact
   D. disregard the comment since the client was probably exhausted and not thinking clearly

   3.____

4. A client who is being interviewed insists on certain facts. The interviewer knows that these statements are incorrect.
   In regard to the rest of the client's statements, the interviewer is MOST justified to
   A. disregard any information the client gives which cannot be verified
   B. try to discover other misstatements by confronting the client with the discrepancy
   C. consider everything else which the client has said as the truth unless proved otherwise
   D. ask the client to prove his statements

5. Immediately after the interviewer identifies himself to a client, she says in a hysterical voice that he is not to be trusted.
   Of the following, the BEST course of action for the interviewer to follow would be to
   A. tell the woman sternly that if she does not stay calm, he will leave
   B. assure the woman that there is no cause to worry
   C. ignore the woman until she becomes quiet
   D. ask the woman to explain her problem

6. Assume that you are an interviewer and that one of your interviewees has asked you for advice on dealing with a personal problem.
   Of the following, the BEST action for you to take is to
   A. tell him about a similar problem which you know worked out well
   B. advise him not to worry
   C. explain that the problem is quite a usual one and that the situation will be brighter soon
   D. give no opinion and change the subject when practicable

7. All of the following are generally good approaches for an interviewer to use in order to improve his interviews EXCEPT
   A. developing a routine approach so that interviews can be standardized
   B. comparing his procedure with that of others engaged in similar work
   C. reviewing each interview critically, picking out one or two weak points to concentrate on improving
   D. comparing his own more successful and less successful interviews

8. Assume that a supervisor suggests at a staff meeting that digital recorders be provided for interviewers. Following are four arguments *against* the use of digital recorders that are raised by other members of the staff that might be valid:
   I. Recorded interviews provide too much unnecessary information
   II. Recorded interviews provide no record of manner or gestures
   III. Digital recorders are too cumbersome and difficult for the average supervisor to manage
   IV. Digital recorders may inhibit the interviewee

Which one of the following choices MOST accurately classifies the above into those which are generally *invalid* and those which are *not*?
A. I and II are generally valid, but III and IV are not.
B. IV is generally valid, but I, II, and III are not.
C. I, II, and IV are generally valid, but III is not.
D. I, II, III, and IV are generally valid.

9. During an interview, the PRIMARY advantage of the technique of using questions as opposed to allowing the interviewee to talk freely is that questioning
   A. gives the interviewer greater control
   B. provides a more complete picture
   C. makes the interviewee more relaxed
   D. decreases the opportunity for exaggeration

10. Assume that, in conducting an interview, an interviewer takes into consideration the age, sex, education, and background of the subject.
    This practice is GENERALLY considered
    A. *undesirable*, mainly because an interviewer may be prejudiced by such factors
    B. *desirable*, mainly because these are factors which might influence a person's response to certain questions
    C. *undesirable*, mainly because these factors rarely have any bearing on the matter being investigated
    D. *desirable*, mainly because certain categories of people answer certain questions in the same way

11. If a client should begin to tell his life story during an interview, the BEST course of action for an interviewer to take is to
    A. interrupt immediately and insist that they return to business
    B. listen attentively until the client finishes and then ask if they can return to the subject
    C. pretend to have other business and come back later to see the client
    D. interrupt politely at an appropriate point and direct the client's attention to the subject

12. An interviewer who is trying to discover the circumstances surrounding a client's accident would be MOST successful during an interview if he avoided questions which
    A. lead the client to discuss the matter in detail
    B. can easily be answered by either "yes" or "no"
    C. ask for specific information
    D. may be embarrassing or annoying to the client

13. A client being interviewed may develop an emotional reaction (positive or negative) toward the interviewer.
    The BEST attitude for the interviewer to take toward such feelings is that they are
    A. *inevitable*; they should be accepted but kept under control
    B. *unusual*; they should be treated impersonally

C. *obstructive*; they should be resisted at all costs
D. *abnormal*; they should be eliminated as soon as possible

14. Encouraging the client being interviewed to talk freely at first is a technique that is supported by all of the following reasons EXCEPT that it
    A. tends to counteract any preconceived ideas that the interviewer may have entertained about the client
    B. gives the interviewer a chance to learn the best method of approach to obtain additional information
    C. inhibits the client from looking to the interviewer for support and advice
    D. allows the client to reveal the answers to many questions before they are asked

15. Of the following, generally the MOST effective way for an interviewer to assure full cooperation from the client he is interviewing is to
    A. sympathize with the client's problems and assure him of concern
    B. tell a few jokes before beginning to ask questions
    C. convince the patient that the answers to the questions will help him as well as the interviewer
    D. arrange the interview when the client feels best

16. Since many elderly people are bewildered and helpless when interviewed, special consideration should be given to them.
    Of the following, the BEST way for an interviewer to *initially* approach elderly clients who express anxiety and fear is to
    A. assure them that they have nothing to worry about
    B. listen patiently and show interest in them
    C. point out the specific course of action that is best for them
    D. explain to them that many people have overcome much greater difficulties

17. Assume that, in planning an initial interview, an interviewer determines in advance what information is needed in order to fulfill the purpose of the interview.
    Of the following, this procedure usually does NOT
    A. reduce the number of additional interviews required
    B. expedite the processing of the case
    C. improve public opinion of the interviewer's agency
    D. assure the cooperation of the person interviewed

18. Sometimes an interviewer deliberately introduces his own personal interests and opinions into an interview with a client.
    In general, this practice should be considered
    A. *desirable*, primarily because the relationship between client and interviewer becomes social rather than businesslike
    B. *undesirable*, primarily because the client might complain to his supervisor
    C. *desirable*, primarily because the focus of attention is directed toward the client
    D. *undesirable*, primarily because an argument between client and interviewer could result

19. The one of the following types of interviewees who presents the LEAST difficult problem to handle is the person who
    A. answers with a great many qualifications
    B. talks at length about unrelated subjects so that the interviewer cannot ask questions
    C. has difficulty understanding the interviewer's vocabulary
    D. breaks into the middle of sentences and completes them with a meaning of his own

19._____

20. A man being interviewed is entitled to Medicaid, but he refuses to sign up for it because he says he cannot accept any form of welfare.
    Of the following, the BEST course of action for an interviewer to take FIRST is to
    A. try to discover the reason for his feeling this way
    B. tell him that he should be glad financial help is available
    C. explain that others cannot help him if he will not help himself
    D. suggest that he speak to someone who is already on Medicaid

20._____

21. Of the following, the outcome of an interview by an interviewer depend MOST heavily on the
    A. personality of the interviewee
    B. personality of the interviewer
    C. subject matter of the questions asked
    D. interaction between interviewer and interviewee

21._____

22. Some clients being interviewed by an interviewer are primarily interested in making a favorable impression.
    The interviewer should be aware of the fact that such clients are MORE likely than other clients to
    A. try to anticipate the answers the interviewer is looking for
    B. answer all questions openly and frankly
    C. try to assume the role of interviewer
    D. be anxious to get the interview over as quickly as possible

22._____

23. The type of interview which a hospital care interviewer usually conducts is *substantially different* from most interviewing situations in all of the following EXCEPT the
    A. setting   B. kinds of clients
    C. techniques employed D. kinds of problems

23._____

24. During an interview, an interviewer uses a "leading question."
    This type of question is so-called because it *generally*
    A. starts a series of questions about one topic
    B. suggests the answer which the interviewer wants
    C. forms the basis for a following "trick" question
    D. sets, at the beginning, the tone of the interview

24._____

25. An interviewer may face various difficulties when he tries to obtain information from a client.
Of the following, the difficulty which is EASIEST for the interviewer to overcome occurs when a client
   A. is unwilling to reveal the information
   B. misunderstands what information is needed
   C. does not have the information available to him
   D. is unable to coherently give the information requested

25._____

KEY (CORRECT ANSWERS)

1.	C		11.	D
2.	B		12.	B
3.	C		13.	A
4.	C		14.	C
5.	D		15.	C
6.	D		16.	B
7.	A		17.	D
8.	C		18.	D
9.	A		19.	C
10.	B		20.	A

21. D
22. A
23. C
24. B
25. B

TEST 2

DIRECTIONS: Each question or incomplete statement is followed by several suggested answers or completions. Select the one that BEST answers the question or completes the statement. *PRINT THE LETTER OF THE CORRECT ANSWER IN THE SPACE AT THE RIGHT.*

1. Of the following, the MOST appropriate manner for an interviewer to assume during an interview with a client is
    A. authoritarian   B. paternal   C. casual   D. businesslike

2. The systematic study of interviewing theory, principles, and techniques by an interviewer will USUALLY
    A. aid him to act in a depersonalized manner
    B. turn his interviewees into stereotyped affairs
    C. make the people he interviews feel manipulated
    D. give him a basis for critically examining his own practice

3. Compiling in advance a list of general questions to ask a client during an interview is a technique USUALLY considered
    A. *desirable*, chiefly because reference to the list will help keep the interview focused on the important issues
    B. *undesirable*, chiefly because use of such a list will discourage the client from speaking freely
    C. *desirable*, chiefly because the list will serve as a record of what questions were asked
    D. *undesirable*, chiefly because use of such a list will make the interview too mechanical and impersonal

4. The one of the following which is usually of GREATEST importance in winning the cooperation of a person being interviewed and while achieving the purpose of the interview is the interviewer's ability to
    A. gain the confidence of the person being interviewed
    B. stick to the subject of the interview
    C. handle a person who is obviously lying
    D. prevent the person being interviewed from withholding information

5. While interviewing clients, an interviewer should use the technique of interruption, beginning to speak when a client has temporarily paused at the end of a phrase or sentence, in order to
    A. limit the client's ability to voice his objections or complaints
    B. shorten, terminate or redirect a client's response
    C. assert authority when he feels that the client is too conceited
    D. demonstrate to the client that pauses in speech should be avoided

6. An interviewer might gain background information about a client by being aware of the person's speech during an interview.
Which one of the following patterns of speech would offer the LEAST accurate information about a client? The

A. number of slang expressions and the level of vocabulary
B. presence and degree of an accent
C. rate of speech and the audibility level
D. presence of a physical speech defect

7. Suppose that you are interviewing a distressed client who claims that he was just laid off from his job and has no money to pay his rent.
Your FIRST action should be to
   A. ask if he has sought other employment or has other sources of income
   B. express your sympathy but explain that he must pay the rent on time
   C. inquire about the reasons he was laid off from work
   D. try to transfer him to a smaller apartment which he can afford

8. Suppose you have some background information on an applicant whom you are interviewing. During the interview, it appears that the applicant is giving you false information.
The BEST thing for you to do at that point is to
   A. pretend that you are not aware of the written facts and let him continue
   B. tell him what you already know and discuss the discrepancies with him
   C. terminate the interview and make a note that the applicant is untrustworthy
   D. tell him that, because he is making false statements, he will not be eligible for an apartment

9. A Spanish-speaking applicant may want to bring his bilingual child with him to an interview to act as an interpreter.
Which of the following would be LEAST likely to affect the value of an interview in which an applicant's child has act as interpreter?
   A. It may make it undesirable to ask certain questions.
   B. A child may do an inadequate job of interpretation.
   C. A child's answers may indicate his feelings toward his parents.
   D. The applicant may not want to reveal all information in front of his child.

10. Assume you are assigned to interview applicants.
Of the following, which is the BEST attitude for you to take in dealing with applicants?
   A. Assume they will enjoy being interviewed because they believe that you have the power of decision
   B. Expect that they have a history of anti-social behavior in the family, and probe deeply into the social development of family members
   C. Expect that they will try to control the interview, thus you should keep them on the defensive
   D. Assume that they will be polite and cooperative and attempt to secure the information you need in a business-like manner

11. If you are interviewing an applicant who is a minority group member in reference to his eligibility, it would be BEST for you to use language that is
   A. *informal*, using ethnic expressions known to the applicant
   B. *technical*, using the expressions commonly used in the agency

C. *simple*, using words and phrases which laymen understand
D. *formal* to remind the applicant that he is dealing with a government agency

12. When interviewing an applicant to determine his eligibility, it is MOST important to
    A. have a prior mental picture of the typical eligible applicant
    B. conduct the interview strictly according to a previously prepared script
    C. keep in mind the goal of the interview, which is to determine eligibility
    D. get an accurate and detailed account of the applicant's life history

13. The practice of trying to imagine yourself in the applicant's place during an interview is
    A. *good*, mainly because you will be able to evaluate his responses better
    B. *good*, mainly because it will enable you to treat him as a friend rather than as an applicant
    C. *poor*, mainly because it is important for the applicant to see you as an impartial person
    D. *poor*, mainly because it is too time-consuming to do this with each applicant

14. When dealing with clients from different ethnic backgrounds, you should be aware of certain tendencies toward prejudice.
    Which of the following statements is LEAST likely to be valid?
    A. Whites prejudiced against Blacks are more likely to be prejudiced against Hispanics than Whites not prejudiced against Blacks.
    B. The less a White is in competition with Blacks, the less likely he is to be prejudiced against them.
    C. Persons who have moved from one social group to another are likely to retain the attitudes and prejudices of their original social group.
    D. When there are few Blacks or Hispanics in a project, Whites are less likely to be prejudiced against them than when there are many.

15. Of the following, the one who is MOST likely to be a good interviewer of people seeking assistance, is one who
    A. tries to get applicants to apply to another agency instead
    B. believes that it is necessary to get as much pertinent information as possible in order to determine the applicant's real needs
    C. believes that people who seek assistance are likely to have persons with a history of irresponsible behavior in their households
    D. is convinced that there is no need for a request for assistance

KEY (CORRECT ANSWERS)

1.	D	6.	C	11.	C
2.	D	7.	A	12.	C
3.	A	8.	B	13.	A
4.	A	9.	C	14.	C
5.	B	10.	D	15.	B

REPORT WRITING
EXAMINATION SECTION
TEST 1

DIRECTIONS: Each question or incomplete statement is followed by several suggested answers or completions. Select the one that BEST answers the question or completes the statement. *PRINT THE LETTER OF THE CORRECT ANSWER IN THE SPACE AT THE RIGHT.*

Questions 1-4.

DIRECTIONS: Answer Questions 1 through 4 on the basis of the following report which was prepared by a supervisor for inclusion in his agency's annual report.

```
Line #
 1    On Oct. 13, I was assigned to study the salaries paid.
 2    to clerical employees in various titles by the city and by
 3    private industry in the area.
 4    In order to get the data I needed, I called Mr. Johnson at
 5    the Bureau of the Budget and the payroll officers at X Corp.—
 6    a brokerage house, Y Co. —an insurance company, and Z Inc. —
 7    a publishing firm. None of them was available and I had to call
 8    all of them again the next day.
 9    When I finally got the information I needed, I drew up a
10    chart, which is attached. Note that not all of the companies I
11    contacted employed people at all the different levels used in the
12    city service.
13    The conclusions I draw from analyzing this information is
14    as follows: The city's entry-level salary is about average for
15    the region; middle-level salaries are generally higher in the
16    city government plan than in private industry; but salaries at the
17    highest levels in private industry are better than city em-
18    ployees' pay.
```

1. Which of the following criticisms about the style in which this report is written is MOST valid?
   A. It is too informal.
   B. It is too concise.
   C. It is too choppy.
   D. The syntax is too complex.

   1.____

2. Judging from the statements made in the report, the method followed by this employee in performing his research was
   A. *good*; he contacted a representative sample of businesses in the area
   B. *poor*; he should have drawn more definite conclusions
   C. *good*; he was persistent in collecting information
   D. *poor*; he did not make a thorough study

   2.____

3. One sentence in this report contains a grammatical error. This sentence begins on line number
   A. 4 B. 7 C. 10 D. 14

4. The type of information given in this report which should be presented in footnotes or in an appendix is the
   A. purpose of the study
   B. specifics about the businesses contacted
   C. reference to the chart
   D. conclusions drawn by the author

5. The use of a graph to show statistical data in a report is SUPERIOR to a table because it
   A. features approximations
   B. emphasizes facts and relationships more dramatically
   C. presents data more accurately
   D. is easily understood by the average reader

6. Of the following, the degree of formality required of a written report in tone is MOST likely to depend on the
   A. subject matter of the report
   B. frequency of its occurrence
   C. amount of time available for its preparation
   D. audience for whom the report is intended

7. Of the following, a distinguishing characteristic of a written report intended for the head of your agency as compared to a report prepared for a lower-echelon staff member is that the report for the agency head should USUALLY include
   A. considerably more detail, especially statistical data
   B. the essential details in an abbreviated form
   C. all available source material
   D. an annotated bibliography

8. Assume that you are asked to write a lengthy report for use by the administrator of your agency, the subject of which is "The Impact of Proposed New Data Processing Operation on Line Personnel" in your agency. You decide that the *most* appropriate type of report for you to prepare is an analytical report, including recommendations.
   The MAIN reason for your decision is that
   A. the subject of the report is extremely complex
   B. large sums of money are involved
   C. the report is being prepared for the administrator
   D. you intend to include charts and graphs

9. Assume that you are preparing a report based on a survey dealing with the attitudes of employees in Division X regarding proposed new changes in compensating employees for working overtime. Three percent of the respondents to the survey voluntarily offer an unfavorable opinion on the method of assigning overtime work, a question not specifically asked of the employees.
   On the basis of this information, the MOST appropriate and significant of the following comments for you to make in the report with regard to employees' attitudes on assigning overtime work is that
   A. an insignificant percentage of employees dislike the method of assigning overtime work
   B. three percent of the employees in Division X dislike the method of assigning overtime work
   C. three percent of the sample selected for the survey voiced an unfavorable opinion on the method of assigning overtime work
   D. some employees voluntarily voiced negative feelings about the method of assigning overtime work, making it impossible to determine the extent of this attitude

9.____

10. A supervisor should be able to prepare a report that is well-written and unambiguous.
    Of the following sentences that might appear in a report, select the one which communicates MOST clearly the intent of its author.
    A. When your subordinates speak to a group of people, they should be well-informed.
    B. When he asked him to leave, SanMan King told him that he would refuse the request.
    C. Because he is a good worker, Foreman Jefferson assigned Assistant Foreman D'Agostino to replace him.
    D. Each of us is responsible for the actions of our subordinates.

10.____

11. In some reports, especially longer ones, a list of the resources (books, papers, magazines, etc.) used to prepare it is included. This list is called the
    A. accreditation   B. bibliography
    C. summary   D. glossary

11.____

12. Reports are usually divided into several sections, some of which are more necessary than others.
    Of the following, the section which is ABSOLUTELY necessary to include in a report is
    A. a table of contents   B. the body
    C. an index   D. a bibliography

12.____

13. Suppose you are writing a report on an interview you have just completed with a particularly hostile applicant.
    Which of the following BEST describes what you should include in this report?
    A. What you think caused the applicant's hostile attitude during the interview
    B. Specific examples of the applicant's hostile remarks and behavior
    C. The relevant information uncovered during the interview
    D. A recommendation that the applicant's request be denied because of his hostility

14. When including recommendations in a report to your supervisor, which of the following is MOST important for you to do?
    A. Provide several alternative courses of action for each recommendation
    B. First present the supporting evidence, then the recommendations
    C. First present the recommendations, then the supporting evidence
    D. Make sure the recommendations arise logically out of the information in the report

15. It is often necessary that the writer of a report present facts and sufficient arguments to gain acceptance of the points, conclusions, or recommendations set forth in the report.
    Of the following, the LEAST advisable step to take in organizing a report, when such argumentation is the important factor, is a(n)
    A. elaborate expression of personal belief
    B. businesslike discussion of the problem as a whole
    C. orderly arrangement of convincing data
    D. reasonable explanation of the primary issues

16. In some types of reports, visual aids add interest, meaning, and support. They also provide an essential means of effectively communicating the message of the report.
    Of the following, the selection of the suitable visual aids to use with a report is LEAST dependent on the
    A. nature and scope of the report
    B. way in which the aid is to be used
    C. aid used in other reports
    D. prospective readers of the report

17. Visual aids used in a report may be placed either in the text material or in the appendix.
    Deciding where to put a chart, table, or any such aid should depend on the
    A. title of the report   B. purpose of the visual aid
    C. title of the visual aid   D. length of the report

18. A report is often revised several times before final preparation and distribution in an effort to make certain the report meets the needs of the situation for which it is designed.
    Which of the following is the BEST way for the author to be sure that a report covers the areas he intended?

A. Obtain a coworker's opinion
B. Compare it with a content checklist
C. Test it on a subordinate
D. Check his bibliography

19. In which of the following situations is an oral report preferable to a written report? When a(n)
    A. recommendation is being made for a future plan of action
    B. department head requests immediate information
    C. long-standing policy change is made
    D. analysis of complicated statistical data is involved

19.____

20. When an applicant is approved, the supervisor must fill in standard forms with certain information.
    The GREATEST advantage of using standard forms in this situation rather than having the supervisor write the report as he sees fit is that
    A. the report can be acted on quickly
    B. the report can be written without directions from a supervisor
    C. needed information is less likely to be left out of the report
    D. information that is written up this way is more likely to be verified

20.____

21. Assume that it is part of your job to prepare a monthly report for your unit head that eventually goes to the director. The report contains information on the number of applicants you have interviewed that have been approved and the number of applicants you have interviewed that have been turned down.
    Errors on such reports are serious because
    A. you are expected to be able to prove how many applicants you have interviewed each month
    B. accurate statistics are needed for effective management of the department
    C. they may not be discovered before the report is transmitted to the director
    D. they may result in loss to the applicants left out of the report

21.____

22. The frequency with which job reports are submitted should depend MAINLY on
    A. how comprehensive the report has to be
    B. the amount of information in the report
    C. the availability of an experienced man to write the report
    D. the importance of changes in the information included in the report

22.____

23. The CHIEF purpose in preparing an outline for a report is usually to insure that
    A. the report will be grammatically correct
    B. every point will be given equal emphasis
    C. principal and secondary points will be properly integrated
    D. the language of the report will be of the same level and include the same technical terms

23.____

24. The MAIN reason for requiring written job reports is to
    A. avoid the necessity of oral orders
    B. develop better methods of doing the work
    C. provide a permanent record of what was done
    D. increase the amount of work that can be done

25. Assume you are recommending in a report to your supervisor that a radical change in a standard maintenance procedure should be adopted.
    Of the following, the MOST important information to be included in this report is
    A. a list of the reasons for making this change
    B. the names of others who favor the change
    C. a complete description of the present procedure
    D. amount of training time needed for the new procedure

KEY (CORRECT ANSWERS)

1.	A		11.	B
2.	D		12.	B
3.	D		13.	C
4.	B		14.	D
5.	B		15.	A
6.	D		16.	C
7.	B		17.	B
8.	A		18.	B
9.	D		19.	B
10.	D		20.	C

21. B
22. D
23. C
24. C
25. A

TEST 2

DIRECTIONS: Each question or incomplete statement is followed by several suggested answers or completions. Select the one that BEST answers the question or completes the statement. *PRINT THE LETTER OF THE CORRECT ANSWER IN THE SPACE AT THE RIGHT.*

1. It is often necessary that the writer of a report present facts and sufficient arguments to gain acceptance of the points, conclusions, or recommendations set forth in the report.
   Of the following, the LEAST advisable step to take in organizing a report, when such argumentation is the important factor, is a(n)
   A. elaborate expression of personal belief
   B. businesslike discussion of the problem as a whole
   C. orderly arrangement of convincing data
   D. reasonable explanation of the primary issues

   1.____

2. Of the following, the factor which is generally considered to be LEAST characteristic of a good control report is that it
   A. stresses performance that adheres to standard rather than emphasizing the exception
   B. supplies information intended to serve as the basis for corrective action
   C. provides feedback for the planning process
   D. includes data that reflect trends as well as current status

   2.____

3. An administrative assistant has been asked by his superior to write a concise, factual report with objective conclusions and recommendations based on facts assembled by other researchers.
   Of the following factors, the administrative assistant should give LEAST consideration to
   A. the educational level of the person or persons for whom the report is being prepared
   B. the use to be made of the report
   C. the complexity of the problem
   D. his own feelings about the importance of the problem

   3.____

4. When making a written report, it is often recommended that the findings or conclusions be presented near the beginning of the report.
   Of the following, the MOST important reason for doing this is that it
   A. facilitates organizing the material clearly
   B. assures that all the topics will be covered
   C. avoids unnecessary repetition of ideas
   D. prepares the reader for the facts that will follow

   4.____

5. You have been asked to write a report on methods of hiring and training new employees. Your report is going to be about ten pages long.
   For the convenience of your readers, a brief summary of your findings should
   A. appear at the beginning of your report
   B. be appended to the report as a postscript
   C. be circulated in a separate memo
   D. be inserted in tabular form in the middle of your report

6. In preparing a report, the MAIN reason for writing an outline is usually to
   A. help organize thoughts in a logical sequence
   B. provide a guide for the typing of the report
   C. allow the ultimate user to review the report in advance
   D. ensure that the report is being prepared on schedule

7. The one of the following which is MOST appropriate as a reason for including footnotes in a report is to
   A. correct capitalization
   B. delete passages
   C. improve punctuation
   D. cite references

8. A completed formal report may contain all of the following EXCEPT
   A. a synopsis
   B. a preface
   C. marginal notes
   D. bibliographical references

9. Of the following, the MAIN use of proofreaders' marks is to
   A. explain corrections to be made
   B. indicate that a manuscript has been read and approved
   C. let the reader know who proofread the report
   D. indicate the format of the report

10. Informative, readable, and concise reports have been found to observe the following rules:
    Rule I.   Keep the report short and easy to understand
    Rule II. Vary the length of sentences.
    Rule III. Vary the style of sentences so that, for example, they are not all just subject-verb, subject-verb.
    Consider this hospital laboratory report: The experiment was started in January. The apparatus was put together in six weeks. At that time, the synthesizing process was begun. The synthetic chemicals were separated. Then they were used in tests on patients.
    Which one of the following choices MOST accurately classifies the above rules into those which are violated by this report ad those which are not?
    A. II is violated, but I and III are not.
    B. III is violated, but I and II are not.
    C. II and III are violated, but I is not.
    D. I, II, and III are violated,

Questions 11-13.

DIRECTIONS: Questions 11 through 13 are based on the following example of a report. The report consists of eight numbered sentences, some of which are not consistent with the principles of good report writing.

(1) I interviewed Mrs. Loretta Crawford in Room 424 of County Hospital. (2) She had collapsed on the street and been brought into emergency. (3) She is an attractive woman with many friends judging by the cards she had received. (4) She did not know what her husband's last job had been, or what their present income was. (5) The first thing that Mrs. Crawford said was that she had never worked and that her husband was presently unemployed. (6) She did not know if they had any medical coverage or if they could pay the bill. (7) She said that her husband could not be reached by telephone but that he would be in to see her that afternoon. (8) I left word at the nursing station to be called when he arrived.

11. A good report should be arranged in logical order.
    Which of the following sentences from the report does NOT appear in its proper sequence in the report?
    A. 1   B. 4   C. 7   D. 8

12. Only material that is relevant to the main thought of a report should be included. Which of the following sentences from the report contains material which is LEAST relevant to this report? Sentence
    A. 3   B. 4   C. 6   D. 8

13. Reports should include all essential information.
    Of the following, the MOST important fact that is missing from this report is:
    A. Who was involved in the interview
    B. What was discovered at the interview
    C. When the interview took place
    D. Where the interview took place

Questions 14-15.

DIRECTIONS: Each of Questions 14 and 15 consists of four numbered sentences which constitute a paragraph in a report. They are not in the right order. Choose the numbered arrangement appearing after letter A, B, C, or D which is MOST logical and which BEST expresses the thought of the paragraph.

14. I. Congress made the commitment explicit in the Housing Act of 1949, establishing as a national goal the realization of a decent home and suitable environment for every American family.
    II. The result has been that the goal of decent home and suitable environment is still as far distant as ever for the disadvantaged urban family
    III. In spite of this action by Congress, federal housing programs have continued to be fragmented and grossly under-funded.
    IV. The passage of the National Housing Act signaled a new federal commitment to provide housing for the nation's citizens.

The CORRECT answer is:
A. I, IV, III, II   B. IV, I, III, II   C. IV, I, III, II   D. II, IV, I, III

15. I. The greater expense does not necessarily involve "exploitation," but it is often perceived as exploitative and unfair by those who are aware of the price differences involved, but unaware of operating costs.
    II. Ghetto residents believe they are "exploited" by local merchants, and evidence substantiates some of these beliefs.
    III. However, stores in low-income areas were more likely to be small independents, which could not achieve the economies available to supermarket chains and were, therefore, more likely to charge higher prices, and the customers were more likely to buy smaller-sized packages which are more expensive per unit of measure.
    IV. A study conducted in one city showed that distinctly higher prices were charged for goods sold in ghetto stores than in other areas.

    The CORRECT answer is:
    A. IV, II, I, III   B. IV, I, III, II   C. II, IV, III, I   D. II, III, IV, I

16. In organizing data to be presented in a formal report, the FIRST of the following steps should be
    A. determining the conclusions to be drawn
    B. establishing the time sequence of the data
    C. sorting and arranging like data into groups
    D. evaluating how consistently the data support the recommendations

17. All reports should be prepared with at least one copy so that
    A. there is one copy for your file
    B. there is a copy for your supervisor
    C. the report can be sent to more than one person
    D. the person getting the report can forward a copy to someone else

18. Before turning in a report of an investigation he has made, a supervisor discovers some additional information he did not include in this report. Whether he rewrites this report to include this additional information should PRIMARILY depend on the
    A. importance of the report itself
    B. number of people who will eventually review this report
    C. established policy covering the subject matter of the report
    D. bearing this new information has on the conclusions of the report

KEY (CORRECT ANSWERS)

1.	A	11.	B
2.	A	12.	A
3.	D	13.	C
4.	D	14.	B
5.	A	15.	C
6.	A	16.	C
7.	D	17.	A
8.	C	18.	D
9.	A		
10.	C		

EXAMINATION SECTION
TEST 1

DIRECTIONS: Each question or incomplete statement is followed by several suggested answers or completions. Select the one that BEST answers the question or completes the statement. *PRINT THE LETTER OF THE CORRECT ANSWER IN THE SPACE AT THE RIGHT.*

Questions 1-22.

DIRECTIONS: Read through each group of words. Indicate in the space at the right the letter of the misspelled word.

1. A. miniature B. recession 1.____
   C. accommodate D. supress

2. A. mortgage B. illogical 2.____
   C. fasinate D. pronounce

3. A. calendar B. heros 3.____
   C. ecstasy D. librarian

4. A. initiative B. extraordinary 4.____
   C. villian D. exaggerate

5. A. absence B. sense 5.____
   C. dosn't D. height

6. A. curiosity B. ninety 6.____
   C. truely D. grammar

7. A. amateur B. definate 7.____
   C. meant D. changeable

8. A. excellent B. studioes 8.____
   C. achievement D. weird

9. A. goverment B. description 9.____
   C. sergeant D. desirable

10. A. proceed B. anxious 10.____
    C. neice D. precede

11. A. environment B. omitted 11.____
    C. apparant D. misconstrue

12. A. comparative B. hindrance 12.____
    C. benefited D. unamimous

99

13. A. embarrass B. recommend 13.____
    C. desciple D. argument

14. A. sophomore B. suprintendent 14.____
    C. concievable D. disastrous

15. A. agressive B. questionnaire 15.____
    C. occurred D. rhythm

16. A. peaceable B. conscientious 16.____
    C. redicule D. deterrent

17. A. mischievious B. writing 17.____
    C. competition D. athletics

18. A. auxiliary B. synonymous 18.____
    C. maneuver D. repitition

19. A. existence B. optomistic 19.____
    C. acquitted D. tragedy

20. A. hypocrisy B. parrallel 20.____
    C. exhilaration D. prevalent

21. A. convalesence B. infallible 21.____
    C. destitute D. grotesque

22. A. magnanimity B. asassination 22.____
    C. incorrigible D. pestilence

Questions 23-40.

DIRECTIONS: In Questions 23 through 40, one sentence fragment contains an error in punctuation or capitalization. Indicate the letter of the INCORRECT sentence fragment and place it in the space at the right.

23. A. Despite a year's work 23.____
    B. in a well-equipped laboratory
    C. my Uncle failed to complete his research
    D. now he will never graduate.

24. A. Gene, if you are going to sleep 24.____
    B. all afternoon I will enter
    C. that ladies' golf tournament
    D. sponsored by the Chamber of Commerce.

3 (#1)

25. A. Seeing the cat slink toward the barn,
    B. the farmer's wife jumped off the
    C. ladder picked up a broom, and began
    D. shouting at the top of her voice.

26. A. Extending over southeast Idaho and
    B. northwest Wyoming, the Tetons
    C. are noted for their height; however the
    D. highest peak is actually under 14,000 feet.

27. A. "Sarah, can you recall the name
    B. of the English queen
    C. who supposedly said, 'We are not
    D. amused?"

28. A. My aunt's graduation present to me
    B. cost, I imagine more than she could
    C. actually afford. It's a
    D. Swiss watch with numerous features.

29. A. On the left are examples of buildings
    B. from the Classical Period; two temples
    C. one of which was dedicated to Zeus; the
    D. Agora, a marketplace; and a large arch.

30. A. Tired of sonic booms, the people who
    B. live near Springfield's Municipal Airport
    C. formed an anti noise organization
    D. with the amusing name of Sound Off.

31. A. "Joe, Mrs. Sweeney said, "your family
    B. arrives Sunday. Since you'll be in
    C. the Labor Day parade, we could ask Mr.
    D. Krohn, who has a big car, to meet them."

32. A. The plumber emerged from the basement and
    B. said, "Mr. Cohen I found the trouble in
    C. your water heater. Could you move those
    D. Schwinn bikes out of my way?"

33. A. The President walked slowly to the
    B. podium, bowed to Edward Everett Hale
    C. the other speaker, and began his formal address:
    D. "Fourscore and seven years ago...."

34. A. Mr. Fontana, I hope, will arrive before
    B. the beginning of the ceremonies; however,
    C. if his plane is delayed, I have a substitute
    D. speaker who can be here at a moments' notice.

25.____
26.____
27.____
28.____
29.____
30.____
31.____
32.____
33.____
34.____

35. A. Gladys wedding dress, a satin creation,
     B. lay crumpled on the floor; her veil,
     C. torn and streaked, lay nearby. "Jilted!"
     D. shrieked Gladys. She was clearly annoyed.

36. A. Although it is poor grammar, the word
     B. hopefully has become television's newest
     C. pet expression; I hope (to use the correct
     D. form) that it will soon pass from favor.

37. A.   Plaza Apartment Hotel
     B.   103 Tower road
     C.   Hampstead, Iowa 52025
     D.   March 13, 2021

38. A. Circulation Department
     B. British History Illustrated
     C. 3000 Walnut Street
     D. Boulder Colorado 80302

39. A. Dear Sirs:
     B. Last spring I ordered a subscription to your
     C. magazine. I had read and enjoyed the May
     D. issue containing the article titled "kings."

40. A. I have not however, received a
     B. single issue. Will you check this?
     C. Sincerely,
     D. Maria Herrera

Questions 41-70.

DIRECTIONS: Questions 41 through 70 represent common grammatical concerns: subject-verb agreement, appropriate use of pronouns, and appropriate use of verbs. Read each sentence and indicate the letter of the grammatically CORRECT answer in the space at the right.

41. THE REIVERS, one of William Faulkner's last works, _____ made into a movie starring Steve McQueen.
    A. has been   B. have been   C. are being   D. were

42. He _____ on the ground, his eyes fastened on an ant slowly pushing a morsel of food toward the ant hill.
    A. layed   B. laid   C. had laid   D. lay

43. Nobody in the tri-cities _____ to admit that a flood could be disastrous.
    A. are willing   B. have been willing
    C. is willing   D. were willing

44. "_____," the senator asked, "have you convinced to run against the incumbent?"
    A. Who B. Whom C. Whomever D. Womsoever

45. Of all the psychology courses that I took, Statistics 101 _____ the most demanding.
    A. was B. are C. is D. were

46. Neither the conductor nor the orchestra members _____ the music to be applauded so enthusiastically.
    A. were expecting
    B. was expecting
    C. is expected
    D. has been expecting

47. The requirements for admission to the Lettermen's Club _____ posted outside the athletic director's office for months.
    A. was B. was being C. has been D. have been

48. Please give me a list of the people _____ to compete in the kayak race.
    A. whom you think have planned
    B. who you think has planned
    C. who you think is planning
    D. who you think are planning

49. I saw Eloise and Abelard earlier today; _____ were riding around in a fancy 1956 MG.
    A. she and him B. her and him C. she and he D. her and he

50. If you _____ the trunk in the attic, I'll unpack it later today.
    A. can sit
    B. are able to sit
    C. can set
    D. have sat

51. _____ all of the flour been used, or may I borrow three cups?
    A. Have B. Has C. Is D. Could

52. In exasperation, the cycle shop's owner suggested that _____ there too long.
    A. us boys were
    B. we boys were
    C. us boys had been
    D. we boys had been

53. Idleness as well as money _____ the root of all evil.
    A. have been
    B. were to have been
    C. is
    D. are

54. Only the string players from the quartet—Gregory, Isaac, _____—remained after the concert to answer questions.
    A. him, and I
    B. he, and I
    C. him, and me
    D. he, and me

55. Of all the antiques that _____ for sale, Gertrude chose to buy a stupid glass thimble.
    A. was
    B. is
    C. would have
    D. were

56. The detective snapped, "Don't confuse me with theories about _____ you believe committed the crime!"
   A. who   B. whom   C. whomever   D. which

57. _____ when we first called, we might have avoided our present predicament.
   A. The plumber's coming
   B. If the plumber would have come
   C. If the plumber had come
   D. If the plumber was to have come

58. We thought the sun _____ in the north until we discovered that our compass was defective.
   A. had rose
   B. had risen
   C. had rised
   D. had raised

59. Each play of Shakespeare's _____ more than _____ share of memorable characters.
   A. contain its
   B. contains; its
   C. contains; it's
   D. contain; their

60. Our English teacher suggested to _____ seniors that either Tolstoy or Dickens _____ the outstanding novelist of the nineteenth century.
   A. we; was considered
   B. we; were considered
   C. us; was considered
   D. us; were considered

61. Sherlock Holmes, together with his great friend and companion Dr. Watson, _____ to aid the woman _____ had stumbled into the room.
   A. has agreed; who
   B. have agreed; whom
   C. has agreed; whom
   D. have agreed; who

62. Several of the deer _____ when they spotted my backpack _____ open in the meadow.
   A. was frightened; laying
   B. were frightened; lying
   C. were frightened; laying
   D. was frightened; lying

63. After the Scholarship Committee announces _____ selection, hysterics often _____.
   A. it's; occur
   B. its; occur
   C. their; occur
   D. their; occurs

64. I _____ the key on the table last night so you and _____ could find it.
   A. layed; her
   B. lay; she
   C. laid; she
   D. laid; her

65. Some of the antelope _____ wandered away from the meadow where the rancher _____ the block of salt.
   A. has; sat
   B. has; set
   C. have; had set
   D. has; sets

66. Macaroni and cheese _____ best to us (that is, to Andy and _____) when Mother adds extra cheddar cheese.
    A. tastes; I
    B. tastes; me
    C. taste; me
    D. taste; I

66._____

67. Frank said, "It must have been _____ called the phone company."
    A. she who
    B. she whom
    C. her who
    D. her whom

67._____

68. The herd _____ moving restlessly at every bolt of lightning; it was either Ted or _____ who saw the beginning of the stampede.
    A. was; me
    B. were; I
    C. was; I
    D. have been; me

68._____

69. The foreman _____ his lateness by saying that his alarm clock _____ until six minutes before eight.
    A. explains; had not rang
    B. explained; has not rung
    C. has explained; rung
    D. explained; hadn't rung

69._____

70. Of all the coaches, Ms. Cox is the only one who _____ that Sherry dives more gracefully than _____.
    A. is always saying; I
    B. is always saying; me
    C. are always saying; I
    D. were always saying; me

70._____

Questions 71-90.

DIRECTIONS: Choose the word in Questions 71 through 90 that is MOST opposite in meaning to the italicized word.

71. *fact*
    A. statistic
    B. statement
    C. incredible
    D. conjecture

71._____

72. *stiff*
    A. fastidious
    B. babble
    C. supple
    D. apprehensive

72._____

73. *blunt*
    A. concise
    B. tactful
    C. artistic
    D. humble

73._____

74. *foreign*
    A. pertinent
    B. comely
    C. strange
    D. scrupulous

74._____

75. *anger*
    A. infer
    B. pacify
    C. taint
    D. revile

75._____

76. *frank*
    A. earnest
    B. reticent
    C. post
    D. expensive

76._____

77. *secure*
    A. precarious   B. acquire   C. moderate   D. frenzied

78. *petty*
    A. harmonious
    C. forthright
    B. careful
    D. momentous

79. *concede*
    A. dispute
    C. subvert
    B. reciprocate
    D. propagate

80. *benefit*
    A. liquidation
    C. detriment
    B. bazaar
    D. profit

81. *capricious*
    A. preposterous
    C. diabolical
    B. constant
    D. careless

82. *boisterous*
    A. devious   B. valiant   C. girlish   D. taciturn

83. *harmony*
    A. congruence   B. discord   C. chagrin   D. melody

84. *laudable*
    A. auspicious
    C. acclaimed
    B. despicable
    D. doubtful

85. *adherent*
    A. partisan   B. stoic   C. renegade   D. recluse

86. *exuberant*
    A. frail   B. corpulent   C. austere   D. bigot

87. *spurn*
    A. accede   B. flail   C. efface   D. annihilate

88. *spontaneous*
    A. hapless
    C. intentional
    B. corrosive
    D. willful

89. *disparage*
    A. abolish   B. exude   C. incriminate   D. extol

90. *timorous*
    A. succinct   B. chaste   C. audacious   D. insouciant

KEY (CORRECT ANSWERS)

1. D	21. A	41. A	61. A	81. B
2. C	22. B	42. D	62.	82. D
3. B	23. C	43. C	63. B	83. B
4. C	24. B	44. B	64. C	84. B
5. C	25. C	45. A	65. C	85. C
6. C	26. C	46. A	66. B	86. C
7. B	27. D	47. D	67. A	87. A
8. B	28. B	48. A	68. C	88. C
9. A	29. B	49. C	69. D	89. D
10. C	30. C	50. C	70. A	90. C
11. C	31. A	51. B	71. D	
12. D	32. B	52. D	72. C	
13. C	33. B	53. C	73. B	
14. C	34. D	54. B	74. A	
15. A	35. A	55. D	75. B	
16. C	36. B	56. B	76. B	
17. A	37. B	57. C	77. A	
18. D	38. D	58. B	78. D	
19. B	39. D	59. B	79. A	
20. B	40. A	60. C	80. C	

EXAMINATION SECTION
TEST 1

DIRECTIONS: Each question or incomplete statement is followed by several suggested answers or completions. Select the one that BEST answers the question or completes the statement.

Questions 1-17.

DIRECTIONS: In each of the following groups of sentences, there are three sentences which are correct and one which is incorrect because it contains an error in grammar, usage, diction, or punctuation. Indicate the letter of the INCORRECT sentence.

1. A. The business was organized under the name of Allen & Co.
   B. The price of admission was two dollars.
   C. The news was brought to Mr. Walters.
   D. There are less slips to be checked today than there were yesterday.

2. A. He only wants you to go with him; consequently I would be in the way.
   B. Whom do you think I saw on my way to lunch today?
   C. I am very much pleased with the work you are doing in my office.
   D. I think he is better than anyone else in his class.

3. A. I do not believe in his going so far away from home.
   B. She dresses exactly like her sister does.
   C. Neither Flora nor I are going to the movies tonight.
   D. The reason for my lateness is that the train was derailed.

4. A. I cannot understand its being on the bottom shelf because I remember putting it on the top shelf.
   B. If you do not agree with the statement above, please put a check next to it.
   C. We were both chosen to represent the association.
   D. The doctor assured us that she would not have to be operated.

5. A. Near the desk stand three chairs.
   B. How many crates of oranges were delivered?
   C. Where's your coat and hat?
   D. Either you or your mother is wrong.

6. A. She attacked the proposal with bitter words.
   B. Last year our team beat your team.
   C. The careless child spilled some milk on the table cloth.
   D. For three weeks last summer, Molly stood with her aunt.

7. A. Don't blame me for it.
   B. I have met but four.
   C. Loan me five dollars.
   D. May I leave early tonight?

2 (#1)

8. A. It's time you knew how to divide by two numbers.
    B. Are you sure the bell has rung?
    C. Whose going to prepare the luncheon?
    D. Will it be all right if you are called at ten o'clock?

8._____

9. A. He had a wide knowledge of birds.
    B. New Orleans is further from Seattle than from Camden.
    C. Keats's poetry is characterized by rich imagery.
    D. He objected to several things—the cost, the gaudiness, and the congestion.

9._____

10. A. There was, in the first place, no indication that a crime had been committed.
    B. She is taller than any other member of the class.
    C. She decided to leave the book lay on the table.
    D. Haven't you any film in stock at this time?

10._____

11. A. Why do you still object to him coming with us to the party?
    B. If I were you, I should wait for them.
    C. If I were ten years older, I should like this kind of job.
    D. I shall go if you desire it.

11._____

12. A. Swimming in the pool, the water looked green.
    B. His speech is so precise as to seem affected.
    C. I would like to go overseas.
    D. We read each other's letters.

12._____

13. A. It must be here somewhere.
    B. The reason is that there is no bread.
    C. Of all other cities, New York is the largest.
    D. The sand was very warm at the beach.

13._____

14. A. If he were wealthy, he would build a hospital for the poor.
    B. I shall insist that he obey you.
    C. They saw that it was him.
    D. What kind of cactus is this one?

14._____

15. A. Because they had been trained for emergencies, the assault did not catch them by surprise.
    B. They divided the loot between the four of them in proportion to their efforts.
    C. The number of strikes is gradually diminishing.
    D. Between acts we went out to the lobby for a brief chat.

15._____

16. A. Through a ruse, the prisoners affected their escape from the concentration camp.
    B. Constant esposure to danger has affected his mind.
    C. Her affected airs served to alienate her from her friends.
    D. Her vivacity was an affectation.

16._____

17. A. It is difficult to recollect what life was like before the war.
    B. Will each of the pupils please hand their home work in?
    C. There are fewer serious mistakes in this pamphlet than I had thought.
    D. "Leave Her to Heaven" is the title of a novel by Ben Ames Williams.

17._____

Questions 18-25.

DIRECTIONS: Each of Questions 18 through 25 consists of three sentences lettered A, B, and C. In each of these questions, one of the sentences may contain an error in grammar, sentence structure, or punctuation, or all three sentences may be correct. If one of the sentences in a question contains an error in grammar, sentence structure, or punctuation, write in the space at the right the letter preceding the sentence which contains the error. If all three sentences are correct, write the letter D.

18. A. Mr. Smith appears to be less competent than I in performing these duties. 18.____
    B. The supervisor spoke to the employee, who had made the error, but did not reprimand him.
    C. When he found the book lying on the table, he immediately notified the owner.

19. A. Being locked in the desk, we were certain that the papers would not be taken. 19.____
    B. It wasn't I who dictated the telegram; I believe it was Eleanor.
    C. You should interview whoever comes to the office today.

20. A. The clerk was instructed to set the machine on the table before summoning the manager. 20.____
    B. He said that he was not familiar with those kind of activities.
    C. A box of pencils, in addition to erasers and blotters, was included in the shipment of supplies.

21. A. The supervisor remarked, "Assigning an employee to the proper type of work is not always easy." 21.____
    B. The employer found that each of the applicants were qualified to perform the duties of the position.
    C. Any competent student is permitted to take this course if he obtains the consent of the instructor.

22. A. The prize was awarded to the employee whom the judges believed to be most deserving. 22.____
    B. Since the instructor believes this book is the better of the two, he is recommending it for use in the school.
    C. It was obvious to the employees that the completion of the task by the scheduled date would require their working overtime.

23. A. These reports have been typed by employees who are trained by a capable supervisor. 23.____
    B. This employee is as old, if not older, than any other employee in the department.
    C. Running rapidly down the street, the messenger soon reached the office.

24. A. It is believed, that if these terms are accepted, the building can be constructed at a reasonable cost. 24.____
    B. The typists are seated in the large office; the stenographers, in the small office.
    C. Either the operators or the machines are at fault.

25. A. Mr. Jones, who is the head of the agency, will come today to discuss the plans for the new training program.   25.____
    B. The reason the report is not finished is that the supply of paper is exhausted.
    C. It is now obvious that neither of the two employees is able to handle this type of assignment.

KEY (CORRECT ANSWERS)

1. D
2. A
3. B
4. D
5. C

6. D
7. C
8. C
9. B
10. C

11. A
12. A
13. C
14. C
15. B

16. A
17. B
18. B
19. A
20. B

21. B
22. D
23. B
24. A
25. D

TEST 2

DIRECTIONS: In each of the following groups of sentences, one sentence is incorrect because it includes an error in grammar, usage, sentence structure, diction, capitalization, or punctuation. Indicate the INCORRECT sentence in each group.

1. A. We shall have to leave it to the jury to make a determination of the facts.
   B. His precision resulted in a nice discrimination between their relative merits.
   C. Green vegetables are healthy foods.
   D. We shall attempt to ascertain whether there has been any tampering with the lock.

2. A. Have you made any definitive plans which may be applied to budget preparation?
   B. We planned on taking a walking trip through the mountains.
   C. I would much rather he had called me after we had taken the trip.
   D. Do you believe that he has a predisposition toward that kind of response?

3. A. He carried out the orders with great dispatch but with little effect.
   B. The cook's overbearing manner overawed his employer.
   C. All of us shall partake of the benefits of exercise.
   D. Miss Smith made less errors than the other typists.

4. A. I believe that we are liable to have good weather tomorrow.
   B. From what I could see, I thought he acted like the others.
   C. Perpetual motion is an idea which is not unthinkable.
   D. Many of us taxpayers are displeased with the service.

5. A. She was incredulous when I told her the incredible tale.
   B. She was told that the symptoms would disappear within a week.
   C. If possible, I should like to sit in front of the very tall couple.
   D. Punish whomever disobeys our commands.

6. A. The men were trapped inside the cave for four days.
   B. The man seated in back of me was talking throughout the play.
   C. He told me that he doesn't know whether he will be able to visit us.
   D. Please bring me the pair of scissors from the table.

7. A. He was charged with having committed many larcenous acts.
   B. Material wealth is certainly not something to be dismissed cavalierly.
   C. He is one of those people who do everything promptly.
   D. I hope to be able to retaliate for the assistance you have given me.

8. A. Have you noted the unusual phenomena to be seen in that portion of the heavens?
   B. The data is as accurate as it is possible to make it.
   C. The enormity of the crime was such that we could not comprehend it.
   D. The collection of monies from some clients was long overdue.

9. A. What you are doing is not really different than what I had suggested.
   B. The enormousness of the animal was enough to make her gasp.
   C. The judge brought in a decision which aroused antagonism in the community.
   D. I asked the monitor to take the papers to the principal.

10. A. He talks as if he were tired.
    B. He amended his declaration to include additional income.
    C. I know that he would have succeeded if he had tried.
    D. Whom does Mrs. Jones think wrote the play?

    10._____

11. A. The stone made a very angry bruise on his forearm.
    B. He said to me: "I'm very mad at you."
    C. In all likelihood, we shall be unable to go to the fair.
    D. He would have liked to go to the theatre with us.

    11._____

12. A. The lawyers tried to settle the case out of court.
    B. "Get out of my life!" she cried.
    C. Walking down the road, the lake comes into view.
    D. The loan which I received from the bank helped me to keep the business going.

    12._____

13. A. I shall go with you providing that we return home early.
    B. He has been providing us with excellent baked goods for many years.
    C. It has been proved, to my satisfaction, to be correct.
    D. Whether we go or not is for you to decide.

    13._____

14. A. He does not seem able to present a logical and convincing argument.
    B. Each of the goaltenders was trying to protect his respective cage.
    C. He said, "I shall go there directly."
    D. The reason he was late was on account of the delay in transportation.

    14._____

15. A. Her mien revealed her abhorrence of his actions.
    B. She used a great deal of rope so it would not come apart.
    C. After he had lived among them, he found much to admire in their way of life.
    D. He waited patiently for the fish to snatch at the bait.

    15._____

16. A. As a result of constant exposure to the elements, he took sick and required medical attention.
    B. Although the automobile is very old, we think it can still be used for a long trip.
    C. He purchased all the supplies she requested with one exception.
    D. He has repeated the story so frequently that I think he has begun to believe it.

    16._____

17. A. It is the noise made by the crickets that you hear.
    B. She told us that she would be at home on Sunday.
    C. She said, "If I'm not there on time, don't wait on me."
    D. Please try to maintain a cheerful disposition under any and all provocations.

    17._____

18. A. Who is the tallest boy in the class?
    B. Where shall I look to find a similar kind of stone?
    C. The horse took the jumps with a great deal of ease.
    D. He is as good, if not better than, any other jumper in the country.

    18._____

19. A. Which of the two machines would be the most practical?
    B. All of us are entitled to a reply if we are to determine whether you should remain as a member of the club.
    C. Everyone who was listening got to his feet and applauded.
    D. There was no indication from his actions that he knew he was wrong.

    19._____

20. A. I beg leave to call upon you in case of emergency.
     B. Do not deter me from carrying out the demands of my office.
     C. Please see me irregardless of the time of day.
     D. The intrepid captain shouted: "Into the fray!"

     20._____

21. A. The teacher asked me whether she could lend the book from me.
     B. You are not permitted to enter the public address system control room while an announcement is being made.
     C. The mother announced loudly that she was going to the district office to find out whether we could refuse to accept her daughter.
     D. It was my opinion that the salesman arrived at a most inopportune time to demonstrate his machine.

     21._____

22. A. Perhaps we can eliminate any possibility of a misunderstanding by placing a special notice on the bulletin board.
     B. The heavy snow storm caused a noticeable drop in student attendance.
     C. We received two different relays, due to the fact that both the district office and the division office sent out separate notices.
     D. Nevertheless, I urge you to prepare for the regular examination by taking the required courses.

     22._____

23. A. By rotating the secretaries' tasks, we should be able to train the entire office staff in all duties.
     B. The boy who had fallen told me that he felt alright, so that I didn't make out an accident report.
     C. The flowers that the secretary had brought added a delightful touch of color to the office.
     D. We shall have to work fast to complete the task before the deadline.

     23._____

24. A. The telephone caller said that he was the boy's father, but his voice sounded immature.
     B. There are very few situations which would require that we close the office and send the staff home early.
     C. Although a packing slip accompanied the package, we had not received an invoice.
     D. The parent claimed that the child had been in school, but the roll book indicated that the boy had been absent from school.

     24._____

25. A. Needless to say, I could not grant the parent her request to see the teacher immediately since the teacher was teaching a class.
     B. The small boy entered the office crying bitterly, and he refused to tell me the cause of his tears.
     C. In describing her son, the mother told me that he was smaller than any boy in his class.
     D. By holding teachers' checks until after lunch, you prevent many teachers from getting to the bank.

     25._____

KEY (CORRECT ANSWERS)

1.	C	11.	B
2.	B	12.	C
3.	D	13.	A
4.	A	14.	D
5.	D	15.	B
6.	B	16.	A
7.	D	17.	C
8.	B	18.	D
9.	A	19.	A
10.	D	20.	C

21. A
22. C
23. B
24. D
25. C

TEST 3

DIRECTIONS: In each of the following groups of sentences, one of the four sentences contains one or more errors in grammar, sentence structure, English usage, or diction. Select the INCORRECT sentence in each case.

1. A. Protest as much as you like, I shall stick to my plan to the bitter end.
   B. It took two men to lift the refrigerator off of the truck.
   C. The dancer, with her company, her orchestra, and her manager, occupies the sixth floor.
   D. When one has worked with his hands he has really earned his keep.

2. A. The large number of crises among African governments indicate the difficulty of transition to independence.
   B. No sooner had the final bell rung than there was a mad scramble toward the door.
   C. Being as helpful as he could, the traffic policeman offered to send for a mechanic.
   D. They climbed higher that they might reach the little souvenir shop.

3. A. That angry retort of Father's came after long provocation.
   B. The frankness of the book presented a difficult problem as far as advertising it.
   C. It is the glory of Yale that she has many famous men to select from.
   D. The stars of the team were the following: Jones, center Smith, end; and Harris, quarterback.

4. A. Next year we shall nominate whomever we please.
   B. The story is so well told that anything but the author's desired effect is impossible.
   C. My Oldsmobile has a Mercury motor, which makes it hard to shift gears.
   D. He is one of those people who believe in existentialist ideas.

5. A. After my previous experiences, I never expect to come this far again.
   B. I like my present work as preparing the way to my future occupation.
   C. To sit and smoke and think and dream was his idea of gratification.
   D. The snowball of knowledge sweeps relentlessly on, stamping additional rivets into the body of science.

6. A. The student racked his brains back and forth over the algebra problem.
   B. It must be conceded that all the young men adapted themselves to the new regulations.
   C. Formal talks were held between the three great powers in an effort to achieve disarmament.
   D. The librarian felt bad about the damaged encyclopedia.

7. A. The policeman wanted to know if the driver of the car had a license.
   B. Not many of these churches are less than thirty years old.
   C. The athlete failed to break his unofficial world decathlon record by a narrow margin.
   D. How different things appear in Washington than in London.

8. A. The agenda for the next meeting contains several highly important topics.
    B. Stemming from the prelate's remarks was the inference that all was not well at the council.
    C. Because the weight of majority opinion is so great is no reason why a dissenter should remain silent.
    D. The general dominating the conference, there was no danger of chaos erupting.

8._____

9. A. Our company, which has thousands of employees, rates Jones one of its best men.
    B. That wars go on may be considered somewhat of an inherited curse for posterity to bear.
    C. Either Italian dressing or mayonnaise goes well with lettuce hearts.
    D. Granted that he had the best intentions, his conduct was not above reproach.

9._____

10. A. There are two "i's" and two "e's" in privilege.
    B. There is no use in Harry's brother saying anything about the situation.
    C. I, not you, am to blame for the condition of this desk.
    D. By relentless logic the group was lead to accept the statements of the eloquent stranger.

10._____

11. A. "It is one of those cars that go faster than 90 miles an hour," said the salesman.
    B. Elementary school children are not the only ones who are tardy; it is also true of high school and college students.
    C. My handsome brother who is in college writes that he is "having a wonderful time"; he is, however, not doing too well scholastically.
    D. A number of clerks were drinking coffee during the coffee break; the number of cups they drank was unbelievable.

11._____

12. A. He asked what had caused the accident. She replied that she did not know since she had not been present when it had occurred.
    B. The new party headed by Prime Minister Wilson advocated government for the people, not by the people.
    C. Five hundred yards of cloth are sufficient to do the work satisfactorily, and I plan to work continually until I finish.
    D. She thought it would be all right for her to do the work in advance of the due date owing to the fact that none of the machines was being used by others.

12._____

13. A. "Oh! please stop that," he said; but when he looked up, they were nowhere to be seen.
    B. The president of the company often told us workers of his experiences as a penniless, untrained beginner forty years ago.
    C. The family showed its approval of the plan and decided to leave for Detroit, Michigan, on May 18th, or, if delay was unavoidable, on May 25th.
    D. "I'm not buying," he said, "it's too expensive.

13._____

14. A. We expect in the next decade to more than hold our own in our race to the moon.
    B. The teachers who have been considering the annual promotion plan today gave their report to the principal.
    C. You are likely to find him sitting beside the brook in the park.
    D. I shall have eaten by the time we go if my plans proceed according to schedule.

14._____

15. A. If you must know — of course, however, this is a secret — Billy just asked to borrow my car.
    B. The job is over with, and neither my wife nor my children will ever persuade me to do it again.
    C. You ought not to have said what you said, and I suggest that you apologize at once.
    D. His friends had begun to understand how much he had done for the organization, but then they seemed to forget everything.

15.____

16. A. Unlike Bill and me, Ted looks really good in a stylish suit.
    B. They have good teachers in our high schools; therefore, I plan to become a high school teacher.
    C. Do you remember the name of the book? the author? the copyright date? the name of the publisher? of the editor?
    D. The secretary and treasurer of the firm intends to hold a meeting with his president within a week or two.

16.____

17. A. Foreign films may be interesting, but I do not see them often. I usually prefer listening to music.
    B. Court reporting has always fascinated me, but last spring I went to a lecture by a famous reporter. Then I made up my mind to be a reporter.
    C. Haven't I asked you a hundred times to take the damaged typewriter to the repair shop which is in the store next to Jones's Candy Store?
    D. Your typewriter should be kept absolutely clean and should be dusted as soon as you have completed your day's work.

17.____

18. A. The salesmen felt very pleased when they heard the manager say that their sales for the month of July, August, and September were much higher than that for the same months the previous year.
    B. Four hundred dollars is too much to pay for these typewriters; I therefore suggest that you do some additional shopping before you make a final decision.
    C. John said that he had swum around the lake three times and that he was now eligible for his swimming certificate.
    D. I recently read "Trade Winds" in The Saturday Review.

18.____

19. A. Neither being sufficiently prepared for it, both brothers had to apply for additional training at the technical school.
    B. The question was laid before them, and after weeks of argument it was still unsettled.
    C. If all goes satisfactorily — and why shouldn't it? — we shall be in Europe before the middle of May
    D. In his first year he was only an office boy, and in his fifth year he was president of the company.

19.____

20. A. Of all my friends he is the one on whom I can most surely depend.
    B. We value the Constitution because of it's guarantees to freedom.
    C. The audience was deeply stirred by the actor's performance.
    D. Give the book to whoever comes into the room first.

20.____

21. A. Everything was in order: the paper rules, the pencils sharpened, the chairs placed.
    B. Neither John nor Peter were able to attend the reception.
    C. In April the streets which had been damaged by cold weather were repaired by the workmen.
    D. You may lend my book to the pupil who you think will enjoy it most.

22. A. He fidgeted, like most children do, while the grown-ups were discussing the problem.
    B. I won't go unless you go with me.
    C. Sitting beside the charred ruins of his cabin, the frontiersman told us the story of the attack.
    D. Certainly there can be no objection to the boys' working on a volunteer basis.

23. A. The congregation was dismissed.
    B. The congregation were deeply moved by the sermon.
    C. What kind of an automobile is that?
    D. His explanation and mine agree.

24. A. There is no danger of him being elected.
    B. There is no doubt of his election.
    C. John and he are to be the speakers.
    D. John and she are to be the speakers.

25. A. Them that honor me I will honor.
    B. They that believe in me shall be rewarded.
    C. Who did you see at the meeting?
    D. Whom are you writing to?

KEY (CORRECT ANSWERS)

1. B
2. A
3. B
4. C
5. D

6. A
7. C
8. C
9. B
10. D

11. B
12. B
13. D
14. D
15. B

16. B
17. B
18. A
19. A
20. B

21. B
22. A
23. C
24. A
25. C

CLERICAL ABILITIES
EXAMINATION SECTION
TEST 1

DIRECTIONS: Each question or incomplete statement is followed by several suggested answers or completions. Select the one that BEST answers the question or completes the statement. *PRINT THE LETTER OF THE CORRECT ANSWER IN THE SPACE AT THE RIGHT.*

Questions 1-4.

DIRECTIONS: Questions 1 through 4 are to be answered on the basis of the information given below.

The most commonly used filing system and the one that is easiest to learn is alphabetical filing. This involves putting records in an A to Z order, according to the letters of the alphabet. The name of a person is filed by using the following order: first, the surname or last name; second, the first name; third, the middle name or middle initial. For example, *Henry C. Young* is filed under *Y* and thereafter under *Young, Henry C.* The name of a company is filed in the same way. For example, *Long Cabinet Co.* is filed under *L* while *John T. Long Cabinet Co.* is filed under *L* and thereafter under *Long, John T. Cabinet Co.*

1. The one of the following which lists the names of persons in the CORRECT alphabetical order is:
   A. Mary Carrie, Helen Carrol, James Carson, John Carter
   B. James Carson, Mary Carrie, John Carter, Helen Carrol
   C. Helen Carrol, James Carson, John Carter, Mary Carrie
   D. John Carter, Helen Carrol, Mary Carrie, James Carson

1._____

2. The one of the following which lists the names of persons in the CORRECT alphabetical order is:
   A. Jones, John C.; Jones, John A.; Jones, John P.; Jones, John K.
   B. Jones, John P.; Jones, John K.; Jones, John C.; Jones, John A.
   C. Jones, John A.; Jones, John C.; Jones, John K.; Jones, John P.
   D. Jones, John K.; Jones, John C.; Jones, John A.; Jones, John P.

2._____

3. The one of the following which lists the names of the companies in the CORRECT alphabetical order is:
   A. Blane Co., Blake Co., Block Co., Blear Co.
   B. Blake Co., Blane Co., Blear Co., Block Co.
   C. Block Co., Blear Co., Blane Co., Blake Co.
   D. Blear Co., Blake Co., Blane Co., Block Co.

3._____

4. You are to return to the file an index card on *Barry C. Wayne Materials and Supplies Co.*
Of the following, the CORRECT alphabetical group that you should return the index card to is

   A. A to G   B. H to M   C. N to S   D. T to Z

4._____

Questions 5-10.

DIRECTIONS: In each of Questions 5 through 10, the names of four people are given. For each question, choose as your answer the one of the four names given which should be filed FIRST according to the usual system of alphabetical filing of names, as described in the following paragraph.

In filing names, you must start with the last name. Names are filed in order of the first letter of the last name, then the second letter, etc. Therefore, BAILY would be filed before BROWN, which would be filed before COLT. A name with fewer letters of the same type comes first, i.e., Smith before Smithe. If the last names are the same, the names are filed alphabetically by the first name. If the first name is an initial, a name with an initial would come before a first name that starts with the same letter as the initial. Therefore, I. BROWN would come before IRA BROWN. Finally, if both last name and first name are the same, the name would be filed alphabetically by the middle name, once again an initial coming before a middle name which starts with the same letter as the initial. If there is no middle name at all, the name would come before those with middle initials or names.

SAMPLE QUESTION: A. Lester Daniels
                                  B. William Dancer
                                  C. Nathan Danzig
                                  D. Dan Lester

The last names beginning with D are filed before the last name beginning with L. Since DANIELS, DANCER, and DANZIG all begin with the same three letters, you must look at the fourth letter of the last name to determine which name should be filed first. C comes before I or Z in the alphabet, so DANCER is filed before DANIELS or DANZIG. Therefore, the answer to the above sample question is B.

5.   A.   Scott Biala
    B.   Mary Byala
    C.   Martin Baylor
    D.   Francis Bauer

5._____

6.   A.   Howard J. Black
    B.   Howard Black
    C.   J. Howard Black
    D.   John H. Black

6._____

7.   A.   Theodora Garth Kingston
    B.   Theadore Barth Kingston
    C.   Thomas Kingston
    D.   Thomas T. Kingston

7._____

8. A. Paulette Mary Huerta
    B. Paul M. Huerta
    C. Paulette L. Huerta
    D. Peter A. Huerta

9. A. Martha Hunt Morgan
    B. Martin Hunt Morgan
    C. Mary H. Morgan
    D. Martine H. Morgan

10. A. James T. Meerschaum
    B. James M. Mershum
    C. James F. Mearshaum
    D. James N. Meshum

Questions 11-14.

DIRECTIONS: Questions 11 through 14 are to be answered SOLELY on the basis of the following information.

You are required to file various documents in file drawers which are labeled according to the following pattern:

DOCUMENTS

MEMOS		LETTERS	
File	Subject	File	Subject
84PM1	(A-L)	84PC1	(A-L)
84PM2	(M-Z)	84PC2	(M-Z)

REPORTS		INQUIRIES	
File	Subject	File	Subject
84PR1	(A-L)	84PQ1	(A-L)
84PR2	(M-Z)	84PQ2	(M-Z)

11. A letter dealing with a burglary should be filed in the drawer labeled
    A. 84PM1 B. 84PC1 C. 84PR1 D. 84PQ2

12. A report on Statistics should be found in the drawer labeled
    A. 84PM1 B. 84PC2 C. 84PR2 D. 84PQS

13. An inquiry is received about parade permit procedures. It should be filed in the drawer labeled
    A. 84PM2 B. 84PC1 C. 84PR1 D. 84PQ2

14. A police officer has a question about a robbery report you filed. You should pull this file from the drawer labeled
    A. 84PM1 B. 84PM2 C. 84PR1 D. 84PR2

Questions 15-22.

DIRECTIONS: Each of Questions 15 through 22 consists of four or six numbered names. For each question, choose the option (A, B, C, or D) which indicates the order in which the names should be filed in accordance with the following filing instructions:
- File alphabetically according to last name, then first name, then middle initial.
- File according to each successive letter within a name.
- When comparing two names in which the letters in the longer name are identical to the corresponding letters in the shorter name, the shorter name is filed first.
- When the last names are the same, initials are always filed before names beginning with the same letter.

15. I. Ralph Robinson
  II. Alfred Ross
  III. Luis Robles
  IV. James Roberts

  The CORRECT filing sequence for the above names should be
  A. IV, II, I, III   B. I, IV, III, II   C. III, IV, I, II   D. IV, I, III, II

16. I. Irwin Goodwin
  II. Inez Gonzalez
  III. Irene Goodman
  IV. Ira S. Goodwin
  V. Ruth I. Goldstein
  VI. M.B. Goodman

  The CORRECT filing sequence for the above names should be
  A. V, II, I, IV, III, VI
  B. V, II, VI, III, IV, I
  C. V, II, III, VI, IV, I
  D. V, II, III, VI, I, IV

17. I. George Allan
  II. Gregory Allen
  III. Gary Allen
  IV. George Allen

  The CORRECT filing sequence for the above names should be
  A. IV, III, I, II   B. I, IV, II, III   C. III, IV, I, II   D. I, III, IV, II

18. I. Simon Kauffman
     II. Leo Kaufman
     III. Robert Kaufmann
     IV. Paul Kauffmann

   The CORRECT filing sequence for the above names should be
   A. I, IV, II, III   B. II, IV, III, I   C. III, II, IV, I   D. I, II, III, IV

19. I. Roberta Williams
     II. Robin Wilson
     III. Roberta Wilson
     IV. Robin Williams

   The CORRECT filing sequence for the above names should be
   A. III, II, IV, I   B. I, IV, III, II   C. I, II, III, IV   D. III, I, II, IV

20. I. Lawrence Shultz
     II. Albert Schultz
     III. Theodore Schwartz
     IV. Thomas Schwarz
     V. Alvin Schultz
     VI. Leonard Shultz

   The CORRECT filing sequence for the above names should be
   A. II, V, III, IV, I, VI
   B. IV, III, V, I, II, VI
   C. II, V, I, VI, III, IV
   D. I, VI, II, V, III, IV

21. I. McArdle
     II. Mayer
     III. Maletz
     IV. McNiff
     V. Meyer
     VI. MacMahon

   The CORRECT filing sequence for the above names should be
   A. I, IV, VI, III, II, V
   B. II, I, IV, VI, III, V
   C. VI, III, II, I, IV, V
   D. VI, III, II, V, I, IV

22. I. Jack E. Johnson
     II. R.H. Jackson
     III. Bertha Jackson
     IV. J.T. Johnson
     V. Ann Johns
     VI. John Jacobs

   The CORRECT filing sequence for the above names should be
   A. II, III, VI, V, IV, I
   B. III, II, VI, V, IV, I
   C. VI, II, III, I, V, IV
   D. III, II, VI, IV, V, I

Questions 23-30.

DIRECTIONS: The code table below shows 10 letters with matching numbers. For each question, there are three sets of letters. Each set of letters is followed by a set of numbers which may or may not match their correct letter according to the code table. For each question, check all three sets of letters and numbers and mark your answer:
    A. if no pairs are correctly matched
    B. if only one pair is correctly matched
    C. if only two pairs are correctly matched
    D. if all three pairs are correctly matched

CODE TABLE

T	M	V	D	S	P	R	G	B	H
1	2	3	4	5	6	7	8	9	0

SAMPLE QUESTION: TMVDSP – 123456
                                RGBHTM – 789011
                                DSPRGB – 256789

    In the sample question above, the first set of numbers correctly match its set of letters. But the second and third pairs contain mistakes. In the second pair, M is correctly matched with number 1. According to the code table, letter M should be correctly matched with number 2. In the third pair, the letter D is incorrectly matched with number 2. According to the code table, letter D should be correctly matched with number 4. Since only one of the pairs is correctly matched, the answer to this sample question is B.

23. RSBMRM – 759262
    GDSRVH – 845730
    VDBRTM - 349713

23.____

24. TGVSDR – 183247
    SMHRDP – 520647
    TRMHSR - 172057

24.____

25. DSPRGM – 456782
    MVDBHT – 234902
    HPMDBT – 062491

25.____

26. BVPTRD – 936184
    GDPHMB – 807029
    GMRHMV - 827032

26.____

27. MGVRSH – 283750
    TRDMBS – 174295
    SPRMGV - 567283

27.____

28. SGBSDM – 489542   28._____
    MGHPTM – 290612
    MPBMHT - 269301

29. TDPBHM – 146902   29._____
    VPBMRS – 369275
    GDMBHM - 842902

30. MVPTBV – 236194   30._____
    PDRTMB – 47128
    BGTMSM - 981232

KEY (CORRECT ANSWERS)

1.	A	11.	B	21.	C
2.	C	12.	C	22.	B
3.	B	13.	D	23.	B
4.	D	14.	D	24.	B
5.	D	15.	D	25.	C
6.	B	16.	C	26.	A
7.	B	17.	D	27.	D
8.	B	18.	A	28.	A
9.	A	19.	B	29.	D
10.	C	20.	A	30.	A

TEST 2

DIRECTIONS: Each question or incomplete statement is followed by several suggested answers or completions. Select the one that BEST answers the question or completes the statement. *PRINT THE LETTER OF THE CORRECT ANSWER IN THE SPACE AT THE RIGHT.*

Questions 1-10.

DIRECTIONS: Questions 1 through 10 each consists of two columns, each containing four lines of names, numbers and/or addresses. For each question, compare the lines in Column I with the lines in Column II to see if they match exactly, and mark your answer A, B, C, or D, according to the following instructions:
    A. all four lines match exactly
    B. only three lines match exactly
    C. only two lines match exactly
    D. only one line matches exactly

<u>COLUMN I</u>   <u>COLUMN II</u>

1.   I. Earl Hodgson   Earl Hodgson   1.____
    II. 1409870   1408970
    III. Shore Ave.   Schore Ave.
    IV. Macon Rd.   Macon Rd.

2.   I. 9671485   9671485   2.____
    II. 470 Astor Court   470 Astor Court
    III. Halprin, Phillip   Halperin, Phillip
    IV. Frank D. Poliseo   Frank D. Poliseo

3.   I. Tandem Associates   Tandom Associates   3.____
    II. 144-17 Northern Blvd.   144-17 Northern Blvd.
    III. Alberta Forchi   Albert Forchi
    IV. Kings Park, NY 10751   Kings Point, NY 10751

4.   I. Bertha C. McCormack   Bertha C. McCormack   4.____
    II. Clayton, MO   Clayton, MO
    III. 976-4242   976-4242
    IV. New City, NY 10951   New City, NY 10951

5.   I. George C. Morill   George C. Morrill   5.____
    II. Columbia, SC 29201   Columbia, SD 29201
    III. Louis Ingham   Louis Ingham
    IV. 3406 Forest Ave.   3406 Forest Ave.

6.   I. 506 S. Elliott Pl.   506 S. Elliott Pl.   6.____
    II. Herbert Hall   Hurbert Hall
    III. 4712 Rockaway Pkway   4712 Rockaway Pkway
    IV. 169 E. 7 St.   169 E. 7 St.

2 (#2)

7. I.   345 Park Ave.   345 Park Pl.   7.____
    II. Colman Oven Corp.   Coleman Oven Corp.
    III. Robert Conte   Robert Conti
    IV. 6179846   6179846

8. I.   Grigori Schierber   Grigori Schierber   8.____
    II. Des Moines, Iowa   Des Moines, Iowa
    III. Gouverneur Hospital   Gouverneur Hospital
    IV. 91-35 Cresskill Pl.   91-35 Cresskill Pl.

9. I.   Jeffery Janssen   Jeffrey Janssen   9.____
    II. 8041071   8041071
    III. 40 Rockefeller Plaza   40 Rockafeller Plaza
    IV. 407 6 St.   406 7 St.

10. I.   5971996   5871996   10.____
    II. 3113 Knickerbocker Ave. 31123 Knickerbocker Ave.
    III. 8434 Boston Post Rd.   8424 Boston Post Rd.
    IV. Penn Station   Penn Station

Questions 11-14.

DIRECTIONS: Questions 11 through 14 are to be answered by looking at the four groups of names and addresses listed below (I, II, III, and IV), and then finding out the number of groups that have their corresponding numbered lies exactly the same.

GROUP I
Line 1.   Richmond General Hospital
Line 2.   Geriatric Clinic
Line 3.   3975 Paerdegat St.
Line 4.   Loudonville, New York 11538

GROUP II
Richman General Hospital
Geriatric Clinic
3975 Peardegat St.
Londonville, New York 11538

GROUP III
Line 1.   Richmond General Hospital
Line 2.   Geriatric Clinic
Line 3.   3795 Paerdegat St.
Line 4.   Loudonville, New York 11358

GROUP IV
Richmend General Hospital
Geriatric Clinic
3975 Paerdegat St.
Loudonville, New York 11538

1. In how many groups is line one exactly the same?   11.____
    A. Two   B. Three   C. Four   D. None

12. In how many groups is line two exactly the same?   12.____
    A. Two   B. Three   C. Four   D. None

13. In how many groups is line three exactly the same?   13.____
    A. Two   B. Three   C. Four   D. None

14. In how many groups is line four exactly the same? 14._____
    A. Two B. Three C. Four D. None

Questions 15-18.

DIRECTIONS: Each of Questions 15 through 18 has two lists of names and addresses. Each list contains three sets of names and addresses. Check each of the three sets in the list on the right to see if they are the same as the corresponding set in the list on the left. Mark your answers:
    A. if none of the sets in the right list are the same as those in the left list
    B. if only one of the sets in the right list is the same as those in the left list
    C. if only two of the sets in the right list are the same as those in the left list
    D. if all three sets in the right list are the same as those in the left list

15. Mary T. Berlinger
    2351 Hampton St.
    Monsey, N.Y. 20117

    Eduardo Benes
    483 Kingston Avenue
    Central Islip, N.Y. 11734

    Alan Carrington Fuchs
    17 Gnarled Hollow Road
    Los Angeles, CA 91635

    Mary T. Berlinger
    2351 Hampton St.
    Monsey, N.Y. 20117

    Eduardo Benes
    473 Kingston Avenue
    Central Islip, N.Y. 11734

    Alan Carrington Fuchs
    17 Gnarled Hollow Road
    Los Angeles, CA 91685

15._____

16. David John Jacobson
    178 34 St. Apt. 4C
    New York, N.Y. 00927

    Ann-Marie Calonella
    7243 South Ridge Blvd.
    Bakersfield, CA 96714

    Pauline M. Thompson
    872 Linden Ave.
    Houston, Texas 70321

    David John Jacobson
    178 53 St. Apt. 4C
    New York, N.Y. 00927

    Ann-Marie Calonella
    7243 South Ridge Blvd.
    Bakersfield, CA 96714

    Pauline M. Thomson
    872 Linden Ave.
    Houston, Texas 70321

16._____

17. Chester LeRoy Masterton
    152 Lacy Rd.
    Kankakee, Ill. 54532

    William Maloney
    S. LaCrosse Pla.
    Wausau, Wisconsin 52136

    Cynthia V. Barnes
    16 Pines Rd.
    Greenpoint, Miss. 20376

    Chester LeRoy Masterson
    152 Lacy Rd.
    Kankakee, Ill. 54532

    William Maloney
    S. LaCross Pla.
    Wausau, Wisconsin 52146

    Cynthia V. Barnes
    16 Pines Rd.
    Greenpoint,, Miss. 20376

17._____

18. Marcel Jean Frontenac   Marcel Jean Frontenac   18.____
     8 Burton On The Water   6 Burton On The Water
     Calender, Me. 01471   Calender, Me. 01471

     J. Scott Marsden   J. Scott Marsden
     174 S. Tipton St.   174 Tipton St.
     Cleveland, Ohio   Cleveland, Ohio

     Lawrence T. Haney   Lawrence T. Haney
     171 McDonough St.   171 McDonough St.
     Decatur, Ga. 31304   Decatur, Ga. 31304

Questions 19-26.

DIRECTIONS: Each of Questions 19 through 26 has two lists of numbers. Each list contains three sets of numbers. Check each of the three sets in the list on the right to see if they are the same as the corresponding set in the list on the left. Mark your answers:
- A. if none of the sets in the right list are the same as those in the left list
- B. if only one of the sets in the right list is the same as those in the left list
- C. if only two of the sets in the right list are the same as those in the left list
- D. if all three sets in the right list are the same as those in the left lists

19. 7354183476   7354983476   19.____
     4474747744   4474747774
     5791430231   57914302311

20. 7143592185   7143892185   20.____
     8344517699   8344518699
     9178531263   9178531263

21. 2572114731   257214731   21.____
     8806835476   8806835476
     8255831246   8255831246

22. 331476853821   331476858621   22.____
     6976658532996   6976655832996
     3766042113715   3766042113745

23. 8806663315   88066633115   23.____
     74477138449   74477138449
     211756663666   211756663666

24. 990006966996   99000696996   24.____
    53022219743   53022219843
    4171171117717   4171171177717

25. 24400222433004   24400222433004   25.____
    5300030055000355   5300030055500355
    20000075532002022   20000075532002022

26. 611166640660001116   61116664066001116   26.____
    7111300117001100733 7111300117001100733
    26666446664476518   26666446664476518

Questions 27-30.

DIRECTIONS: Questions 27 through 30 are to be answered by picking the answer which is in the correct numerical order, from the lowest number to the highest number, in each question.

27. A. 44533, 44518, 44516, 44547   27.____
     B. 44516, 44518, 44533, 44547
     C. 44547, 44533, 44518, 44516
     D. 44518, 44516, 44547, 44533

28. A. 95587, 95593, 95601, 95620   28.____
     B. 95601, 95620, 95587, 95593
     C. 95593, 95587, 95601. 95620
     D. 95620, 95601, 95593, 95587

29. A. 232212, 232208, 232232, 232223   29.____
     B. 232208, 232223, 232212, 232232
     C. 232208, 232212, 232223, 232232
     D. 232223, 232232, 232208, 232208

30. A. 113419, 113521, 113462, 113462   30.____
     B. 113588, 113462, 113521, 113419
     C. 113521, 113588, 113419, 113462
     D. 113419, 113462, 113521, 113588

KEY (CORRECT ANSWERS)

1.	C	11.	A	21.	C
2.	B	12.	C	22.	A
3.	D	13.	A	23.	D
4.	A	14.	A	24.	A
5.	C	15.	C	25.	C
6.	B	16.	B	26.	C
7.	D	17.	B	27.	B
8.	A	18.	B	28.	A
9.	D	19.	B	29.	C
10.	C	20.	B	30.	D

RECORD KEEPING

EXAMINATION SECTION

TEST 1

DIRECTIONS: Each question or incomplete statement is followed by several suggested answers or completions. Select the one that BEST answers the question or completes the statement. *PRINT THE LETTER OF THE CORRECT ANSWER IN THE SPACE AT THE RIGHT.*

Questions 1-15.

DIRECTIONS: Questions 1 through 15 are to be answered on the basis of the following list of company names below. Arrange a file alphabetically, word-by-word, disregarding punctuation, conjunctions, and apostrophes. Then answer the questions.

    A Bee C Reading Materials
    ABCO Parts
    A Better Course for Test Preparation
    AAA Auto Parts Co.
    A-Z Auto Parts, Inc.
    Aabar Books
    Abbey, Joanne
    Boman-Sylvan Law Firm
    BMW Autowerks
    C Q Service Company
    Chappell-Murray, Inc.
    E&E Life Insurance
    Emcrisco
    Gigi Arts
    Gordon, Jon & Associates
    SOS Plumbing
    Schmidt, J.B. Co.

1. Which of these files should appear FIRST?
   A. ABCO Parts
   B. A Bee C Reading Materials
   C. A Better Course for Test Preparation
   D. AAA Auto Parts Co.

    1.____

2. Which of these files should appear SECOND?
   A. A-Z Auto Parts, Inc.
   B. A Bee C Reading Materials
   C. A Better Course for Test Preparation
   D. AAA Auto Parts Co.

    2.____

3. Which of these files should appear THIRD?
   A. ABCO Parts
   B. A Bee C Reading Materials
   C. Aabar Books
   D. AAA Auto Parts Co.

   3.____

4. Which of these files should appear FOURTH?
   A. Aabar Books
   B. ABCO Parts
   C. Abbey, Joanne
   D. AAA Auto Parts Co.

   4.____

5. Which of these files should appear LAST?
   A. Gordon, Jon & Associates
   B. Gigi Arts
   C. Schmidt, J.B. Co.
   D. SOS Plumbing

   5.____

6. Which of these files should appear between A-Z Auto Parts, Inc. and Abbey, Joanne?
   A. A Bee C Reading Materials
   B. AAA Auto Parts Co.
   C. ABCO Parts
   D. A Better Course for Test Preparation

   6.____

7. Which of these files should appear between ABCO Parts and Aabar Books?
   A. A Bee C Reading Materials
   B. Abbey, Joanne
   C. Aabar Books
   D. A-Z Auto Parts

   7.____

8. Which of these files should appear between Abbey, Joanne and Boman-Sylvan Law Firm?
   A. A Better Course for Test Preparation
   B. BMW Autowerks
   C. Chappell-Murray, Inc.
   D. Aabar Books

   8.____

9. Which of these files should appear between Abbey, Joanne and C Q Service?
   A. A-Z Auto Parts, Inc.
   B. BMW Autowerks
   C. Choices A and B
   D. Chappell-Murray, Inc.

   9.____

10. Which of these files should appear between C Q Service Company and Emcrisco?
    A. Chappell-Murray, Inc.
    B. E&E Life Insurance
    C. Gigi Arts
    D. Choices A and B

    10.____

11. Which of these files should NOT appear between C Q Service Company and E&E Life Insurance?
    A. Gordon, Jon & Associates
    B. Emcrisco
    C. Gigi Arts
    D. All of the above

    11.____

12. Which of these files should appear between Chappell-Murray, Inc. and 12._____
Gigi Arts?
    A. C Q Service Inc., E&E Life Insurance, and Emcrisco
    B. Emcrisco, E&E Life Insurance, and Gordon, Jon & Associates
    C. E&E Life Insurance, and Emcrisco
    D. Emcrisco and Gordon, Jon & Associates

13. Which of these files should appear between Gordon, Jon & Associates and 13._____
SOS Plumbing?
    A. Gigi Arts   B. Schmidt, J.B. Co.
    C. Choices A and B   D. None of the above

14. Each of the choices lists the four files in their proper alphabetical order 14._____
EXCEPT
    A. E&E Life Insurance; Gigi Arts; Gordon, Jon & Associates; SOS Plumbing
    B. E&E Life Insurance; Emcrisco; Gigi Arts; SOS Plumbing
    C. Emcrisco; Gordon, Jon & Associates; SOS Plumbing; Schmidt, J.B. Co.
    D. Emcrisco; Gigi Arts; Gordon, Jon & Associates; SOS Plumbing

15. Which of the choices lists the four files in their proper alphabetical order? 15._____
    A. Gigi Arts; Gordon, Jon & Associates; SOS Plumbing; Schmidt, J.B. Co.
    B. Gordon, Jon & Associates; Gigi Arts; Schmidt, J.B. Co.; SOS Plumbing
    C. Gordon, Jon & Associates; Gigi Arts; SOS Plumbing; Schmidt, J.B. Co.
    D. Gigi Arts; Gordon, Jon & Associates; Schmidt, J.B. Co.; SOS Plumbing

16. The alphabetical filing order of two businesses with identical names is 16._____
determined by the
    A. length of time each business has been operating
    B. addresses of the businesses
    C. last name of the company president
    D. no one of the above

17. In an alphabetical filing system, if a business name includes a number, it should 17._____
be
    A. disregarded
    B. considered a number and placed at the end of an alphabetical section
    C. treated as though it were written in words and alphabetized accordingly
    D. considered a number and placed at the beginning of an alphabetical
       section

18. If a business name includes a contraction (such as *don't* or *it's*), how should 18._____
that word be treated in an alphabetical system?
    A. Divide the word into its separate parts and treat it as two words
    B. Ignore the letters that come after the apostrophe
    C. Ignore the word that contains the contraction
    D. Ignore the apostrophe and consider all letters in the contraction

19. In what order should the parts of an address be considered when using an alphabetical filing system? 19.____
    A. City or town; state; street name; house or building number
    B. State; city or town; street name; house or building number
    C. House or building number; street name; city or town; state
    D. Street name; city or town; state

20. A business record should be cross-referenced when a(n) 20.____
    A. organization is known by an abbreviated name
    B. business has a name change because of a sale, incorporation, or other reason
    C. business is known by a *coined* or common name which differs from a dictionary spelling
    D. all of the above

21. A geographical filing system is MOST effective when 21.____
    A. location is more important than name
    B. many names or titles sound alike
    C. dealing with companies who have offices all over the world
    D. filing personal and business files

Questions 22-25.

DIRECTIONS: Questions 22 through 25 are to be answered on the basis of the list of items below, which are to be filed geographically. Organize the items geographically and then answer the questions.

   I. University Press at Berkeley, U.S.
   II. Maria Sanchez, Mexico City, Mexico
   III. Great Expectations Ltd. in London, England
   IV. Justice League, Cape Town, South Africa, Africa
   V. Crown Pearls Ltd. in London, England
   VI. Joseph Prasad in London, England

22. Which of the following arrangements of the items is composed according to the policy of: *Continent, Country, City, Firm or Individual Name*? 22.____
    A. V, III, IV, VI, II, I   B. IV, V, III, VI, II, I
    C. I, IV, V, III, VI, II   D. IV, V, III, VI, I, II

23. Which of the following files is arranged according to the policy of: *Continent, Country, City, Firm or Individual Name*? 23.____
    A. South Africa; Africa; Cape Town; Justice League
    B. Mexico; Mexico City; Maria Sanchez
    C. North America; United States; Berkeley; University Press
    D. England; Europe; London; Prasad, Joseph

24. Which of the following arrangements of the items is composed according to the policy of: *Country, City, Firm or Individual Name*?
    A. V, VI, III, II, IV, I
    B. I, V, VI, III, II, IV
    C. VI, V, III, II, IV, I
    D. V, III, VI, II, IV, I

25. Which of the following files is arranged according to a policy of: *Country, City, Firm or Individual Name*?
    A. England; London; Crown Pearls Ltd.
    B. North America; United States; Berkeley; University Press
    C. Africa; Cape Town; Justice League
    D. Mexico City; Mexico; Maria Sanchez

26. Under which of the following circumstances would a phonetic filing system be MOST effective?
    A. When the person in charge of filing can't spell very well
    B. With large files with names that sound alike
    C. With large files with names that are spelled alike
    D. All of the above

Questions 27-29.

DIRECTIONS: Questions 27 through 29 are to be answered on the basis of the following list of numerical files.

  I. 391-023-100
  II. 361-132-170
  III. 385-732-200
  IV. 381-432-150
  V. 391-632-387
  VI. 361-423-303
  VII. 391-123-271

27. Which of the following arrangements of the files follows a consecutive-digit system?
    A. II, III, IV, I   B. I, V, VII, III   C. II, IV, III, I   D. III, I, V, VII

28. Which of the following arrangements follows a terminal-digit system?
    A. I, VII, II, IV, III
    B. II, I, IV, V, VII
    C. VII, VI, V, IV, III
    D. I, IV, II, III, VII

29. Which of the following lists follows a middle-digit system?
    A. I, VII, II, VI, IV, V, III
    B. I, II, VII, IV, VI, V, III
    C. VII, II, I, III, V, VI, IV
    D. VII, I, II, IV, VI, V, III

Questions 30-31.

DIRECTIONS: Questions 30 and 31 are to be answered on the basis of the following information.

    I. Reconfirm Laura Bates appointment with James Caldecort on December 12 at 9:30 A.M.
    II. Laurence Kinder contact Julia Lucas on August 3 and set up a meeting for week of September 23 at 4 P.M.
    III. John Lutz contact Larry Waverly on August 3 and set up appointment for September 23 at 9:30 A.M.
    IV. Call for tickets for Gerry Stanton August 21 for New Jersey on September 23, flight 143 at 4:43 P.M.

30. A chronological file for the above information would be
    A. IV, III, II, I   B. III, II, IV, I   C. IV, II, III, I   D. III, I, II, IV

31. Using the above information, a chronological file for the date September 23 would be
    A. II, III, IV   B. III, I, IV   C. III, II, IV   D. IV, III, II

Questions 32-34.

DIRECTIONS: Questions 32 through 34 are to be answered on the basis of the following information.

    I. Call Roger Epstein, Ashoke Naipaul, Jon Anderson, and Sara Washingon on April 19 at 1:00 P.M. to set up meeting with Alika D'Ornay for June 6 in New York.
    II. Call Martin Ames before noon on April 19 to confirm afternoon meeting with Bob Greenwood on April 20th.
    III. Set up meeting room at noon for 2:30 P.M. meeting on April 19th.
    IV. Ashley Stanton contact Bob Greenwood at 9:00 A.M. on April 20 and set up meeting for June 6 at 8:30 A.M.
    V. Carol Guiland contact Shelby Van Ness during afternoon of April 20 and set up meeting for June 6 at 10:00 A.M.
    VI. Call airline and reserve tickets on June 6 for Roger Epstein trip to Denver on July 8.
    VII. Meeting at 2:30 P.M. on April 19th.

32. A chronological file for all of the above information would be
    A. II, I, III, VII, V, IV, VI   B. III, VII, II, I, IV, V, VI
    C. III, VII, I, II, V, IV, VI   D. II, III, I, VII, IV, V, VI

33. A chronological file for the date of April 19th would be
    A. II, III, VII, I   B. II, III, I, VII   C. VII, I, III, II   D. III, VII, I, II

34. Add the following information to the file, and then create a chronological file for April 20th: VIII. April 20: 3:00 P.M. meeting between Bob Greenwood and Martin Ames.
    A. IV, V, VIII   B. IV, VIII, V   C. VIII, V, IV   D. V, IV, VIII

34._____

35. The PRIMARY advantage of computer records over a manual system is
    A. speed of retrieval
    B. accuracy
    C. cost
    D. potential file loss

35._____

KEY (CORRECT ANSWERS)

1.	B	11.	D	21.	A	31.	C
2.	C	12.	C	22.	B	32.	D
3.	D	13.	B	23.	C	33.	B
4.	A	14.	C	24.	D	34.	A
5.	D	15.	D	25.	A	35.	A
6.	C	16.	B	26.	B		
7.	B	17.	C	27.	C		
8.	B	18.	D	28.	D		
9.	C	19.	A	29.	A		
10.	D	20.	D	30.	B		

NAME AND NUMBER CHECKING
EXAMINATION SECTION
TEST 1

DIRECTIONS: This test is designed to measure your speed/and accuracy. You are urged to work both quickly and accurately and to do correctly as many lists as you can in the time allowed. The test consists of lists or pairs of names and numbers. Count the number of IDENTICAL pairs in each list. Then, select the correct number, 1, 2, 3, 4, 5, and indicate your choice in the space at the right. Two sample questions are presented for your guidance, together with the correct solutions.

SAMPLE LIST A
Adelphi College – Adelphia College
Braxton Corp – Braxeton Corp.
Wassaic State School – Wassaic State School
Central Islip State Hospital – Central Isllip State Hospital
Greenwich House – Greenwich House

NOTE: There are only two correct pairs—Wassaic State School and Greenwich House. Therefore, the CORRECT answer is 2.

SAMPLE LIST B
78453694 – 78453684
784530 – 784530
533 – 534
67845 – 67845
2368745 – 2368755

NOTE: There are only two correct pairs—784530 and 67845. Therefore, the CORRECT answer is 2.

LIST 1   1.____
    Diagnostic Clinic   – Diagnostic Clinic
    Yorkville Health   – Yorkville Health
    Meinhard Clinic   – Meinhart Clinic
    Corlears Clinic   – Carlears Clinic
    Tremont Diagnostic – Tremont Diagnostic

LIST 2   2.____
    73526   – 73526
    7283627198   – 7283627198
    627   – 637
    728352617283 – 7283526178282
    6281   – 6281

2 (#1)

LIST 3
    Jefferson Clinic   – Jeffersen Clinic
    Mott Haven Center   – Mott Havan Center
    Bronx Hospital   – Bronx Hospital
    Montefiore Hospital   – Montifeore Hospital
    Beth Isreal Hospital   – Beth Israel Hospital

3.____

LIST 4
    936271826   – 936371826
    5271   – 5291
    82637192037   – 82637192037
    527182   – 5271882
    726354256   - 72635456

4.____

LIST 5
    Trinity Hospital   – Trinity Hospital
    Central Harlem   – Centrel Harlem
    St. Luke's Hospital   – St. Lukes' Hospital
    Mt. Sinai Hospital   – Mt. Sinia Hospital
    N.Y. Dispensery   – N.Y. Dispensary

5.____

LIST 6
    725361552637   – 725361555637
    7526378   – 7526377
    6975   – 6975
    82637481028   – 82637481028
    3427   – 3429

6.____

LIST 7
    Misericordia Hospital   – Miseracordia Hospital
    Lebonan Hospital   – Lebanon Hospital
    Gouverneur Hospital   – Gouverner Hospital
    German Polyclinic   – German Policlinic
    French Hospital   – French Hospital

7.____

LIST 8
    8277364933251   – 827364933351
    63728   – 63728
    367281   – 367281
    62733846273   – 6273846293
    62836   - 6283

8.____

LIST 9
    King's County Hospital   – Kings County Hospital
    St. Johns Long Island   – St. John's Long Island
    Bellevue Hospital   – Bellvue Hospital
    Beth David Hospital   – Beth David Hospital
    Samaritan Hospital   – Samariton Hospital

9.____

3 (#1)

LIST 10
    62836454   – 62836455
    42738267   – 42738369
    573829   – 573829
    738291627874   – 738291627874
    725   - 735

10.____

LIST 11
    Bloomingdal Clinic   – Bloomingdale Clinic
    Communitty Hospital – Community Hospital
    Metroplitan Hospital   – Metropoliton Hospital
    Lenox Hill Hospital   – Lonex Hill Hospital
    Lincoln Hospital   – Lincoln Hospital

11.____

LIST 12
    6283364728   – 6283648
    627385   – 627383
    54283902   – 54283602
    63354   – 63354
    7283562781   - 7283562781

12.____

LIST 13
    Sydenham Hospital   – Sydanham Hospital
    Roosevalt Hospital   – Roosevelt Hospital
    Vanderbilt Clinic   – Vanderbild Clinic
    Women's Hospital   – Woman's Hospital
    Flushing Hospital   – Flushing Hospital

13.____

LIST 14
    62738   – 62738
    727355542321   – 72735542321
    263849332   – 263849332
    262837   – 263837
    47382912   - 47382922

14.____

LIST 15
    Episcopal Hospital   – Episcapal Hospital
    Flower Hospital   – Flouer Hospital
    Stuyvesent Clinic   – Stuyvesant Clinic
    Jamaica Clinic   – Jamaica Clinic
    Ridgwood Clinic   – Ridgewood Clinic

15.____

LIST 16
    628367299   – 628367399
    111   – 111
    118293304829   – 1182839489
    4448   – 4448
    333693678   - 333693678

16.____

LIST 17
Arietta Crane Farm — Areitta Crane Farm
Bikur Chilim Home — Bikur Chilom Home
Burke Foundation — Burke Foundation
Blythedale Home — Blythdale Home
Campbell Cottages — Cambell Cottages

17.____

LIST 18
32123 — 32132
273893326783 — 27389326783
473829 — 473829
7382937 — 7383937
3628890122332 - 36289012332

18.____

LIST 19
Caraline Rest — Caroline Rest
Loreto Rest — Loretto Rest
Edgewater Creche — Edgwater Creche
Holiday Farm — Holiday Farm
House of St. Giles — House of st. Giles

19.____

LIST 20
557286777 — 55728677
3678902 — 3678892
1567839 — 1567839
7865434712 — 7865344712
9927382 - 9927382

20.____

LIST 21
Isabella Home — Isabela Home
James A. Moore Home — James A. More Home
The Robin's Nest — The Roben's Nest
Pelham Home — Pelam Home
St. Eleanora's Home — St. Eleanora's Home

21.____

LIST 22
273648293048 — 273648293048
334 — 334
7362536478 — 7362536478
7362819273 — 7362819273
7362 - 7363

22.____

LIST 23
St. Pheobe's Mission — St. Phebe's Mission
Seaside Home — Seaside Home
Speedwell Society — Speedwell Society
Valeria Home — Valera Home
Wiltwyck - Wildwyck

23.____

5 (#1)

LIST 24
   63728   – 63738
   63728192736   – 63728192738
   428   – 458
   62738291527   – 62738291529
   63728192   - 63728192

24.____

LIST 25
   McGaffin   – McGafin
   David Ardslee   – David Ardslee
   Axton Supply   – Axeton Supply Co
   Alice Russell   – Alice Russell
   Dobson Mfg. Co.   – Dobsen Mfg. Co.

25.____

KEY (CORRECT ANSWERS)

1.	3	11.	1
2.	3	12.	2
3.	1	13.	1
4.	1	14.	2
5.	1	15.	1
6.	2	16.	3
7.	1	17.	1
8.	2	18.	1
9.	1	19.	1
10.	2	20.	2

21.	1
22.	4
23.	2
24.	1
25.	2

TEST 2

DIRECTIONS: This test is designed to measure your speed/and accuracy. You are urged to work both quickly and accurately and to do correctly as many lists as you can in the time allowed. The test consists of lists or pairs of names and numbers. Count the number of IDENTICAL pairs in each list. Then, select the correct number, 1, 2, 3, 4, 5, and indicate your choice in the space at the right.

LIST 1
    82637381028   – 82637281028
    928   – 928
    72937281028   – 72937281028
    7362   – 7362
    927382615   – 927382615

1.____

LIST 2
    Albee Theatre   – Albee Theatre
    Lapland Lumber Co. – Laplund Lumber Co.
    Adelphi College   – Adelphi College
    Jones & Son Inc.   – Jones & Sons Inc.
    S.W. Ponds Co.   – S.W. Ponds Co.

2.____

LIST 3
    85345   – 85345
    895643278   – 895643277
    726352   – 726353
    632685   – 632685
    7263524   – 7236524

3.____

LIST 4
    Eagle Library   – Eagle Library
    Dodge Ltd.   – Dodge Co.
    Stromberg Carlson   – Stromberg Carlsen
    Clairice Ling   – Clairice Linng
    Mason Book Co.   – Matson Book Co.

4.____

LIST 5
    66273   – 66273
    629   – 629
    7382517283   – 7382517283
    637281   – 639281
    2738261   – 2788261

5.____

LIST 6
    Robert MacColl   – Robert McColl
    Buick Motor   – Buck Motors
    Murray Bay & Co. Ltd. – Murray Bay Co. Ltd.
    L.T. Ltyle   – L.T. Lyttle
    A.S. Landas   – A.S. Landas

6.____

2 (#2)

LIST 7 7.____
    6271526374890 — 627152637490
    73526189 — 73526189
    5372 — 5392
    637281142 — 63728124
    4783946 — 4783046

LIST 8 8.____
    Tyndall Burke — Tyndell Burke
    W. Briehl — W. Briehl
    Burritt Publishing Co. — Buritt Publishing Co.
    Frederick Breyer & Co. — Frederick Breyer Co.
    Bailey Buulard — Bailey Bullard

LIST 9 9.____
    634 — 634
    16837 — 163837
    273892223678 — 27389223678
    527182 — 527782
    3628901223 — 3629002223

LIST 10 10.____
    Ernest Boas — Ernest Boas
    Rankin Barne — Rankin Barnes
    Edward Appley — Edward Appely
    Camel — Camel
    Caiger Food Co. — Caiger Food Co.

LIST 11 11.____
    6273 — 6273
    322 — 332
    15672839 — 15672839
    63728192637 — 63728192639
    738 — 738

LIST 12 12.____
    Wells Fargo Co. — Wells Fargo Co.
    W.D. Brett — W.D. Britt
    Tassco Co. — Tassko Co.
    Republic Mills — Republic Mill
    R.W. Burnham — R.W. Burhnam

LIST 13 13.____
    7253529152 — 7283529152
    6283 — 6383
    52839102738 — 5283910238
    308 — 398
    82637201927 — 8263720127

3 (#2)

LIST 14
Schumacker Co.	– Shumacker Co.
C.H. Caiger	– C.H. Caiger
Abraham Strauss	– Abram Straus
B.F. Boettjer	– B.F. Boettijer
Cut-Rate Store	– Cut-Rate Stores

14.____

LIST 15
15273826	– 15273826
72537	– 73537
726391027384	– 62639107384
637389	– 627399
725382910	– 725382910

15.____

LIST 16
Hixby Ltd.	– Hixby Lt'd.
S. Reiner	– S. Riener
Reynard Co.	– Reynord Co.
Esso Gassoline Co.	– Esso Gasolene Co.
Belle Brock	– Belle Brock

16.____

LIST 17
7245	– 7245
819263728192	– 819263728172
682537289	– 682537298
789	– 789
82936542891	– 82936542891

17.____

LIST 18
Joseph Cartwright	– Joseph Cartwrite
Foote Food Co.	– Foot Food Co.
Weiman & Held	– Weiman & Held
Sanderson Shoe Co.	– Sandersen Shoe Co.
A.M. Byrne	– A.N. Byrne

18.____

LIST 19
4738267	– 4738277
63728	– 63729
6283628901	– 6283628991
918264	– 918264
263728192037	– 2637728192073

19.____

LIST 20
Exray Laboratories	– Exray Labratories
Curley Toy Co.	– Curly Toy Co.
J. Lauer & Cross	– J. Laeur & Cross
Mireco Brands	– Mireco Brands
Sandor Lorand	– Sandor Larand

20.____

4 (#2)

LIST 21
    607   – 609
    6405   – 6403
    976   – 996
    101267   – 101267
    2065432   – 20965432

21.____

LIST 22
    John Macy & Sons   – John Macy & Son
    Venus Pencil Co.   – Venus Pencil Co.
    Nell McGinnis   – Nell McGinnis
    McCutcheon & Co.   – McCutcheon & Co.
    Sun-Tan Oil   – Sun-Tan Oil

22.____

LIST 23
    703345700   – 703345700
    46754   – 466754
    3367490   – 3367490
    3379   – 3778
    47384   – 47394

23.____

LIST 24
    arthritis   – arthritis
    asthma   – asthma
    endocrine   – endocrene
    gastro-enterological – gastrol-enteralogical
    orthopedic   – orthopedic

24.____

LIST 25
    743829432   – 743828432
    998   – 998
    732816253902   – 732816252902
    46829   – 46830
    7439120249   – 7439210249

25.____

KEY (CORRECT ANSWERS)

1.	4		11.	3
2.	3		12.	1
3.	2		13.	1
4.	1		14.	1
5.	2		15.	2
6.	1		16.	1
7.	2		17.	3
8.	1		18.	1
9.	1		19.	1
10.	3		20.	1

21. 1
22. 4
23. 2
24. 3
25. 1

www.ingramcontent.com/pod-product-compliance
Lightning Source LLC
Chambersburg PA
CBHW080323020526
44117CB00035B/2638